DIRTY VEGAN

Matt Pritchard

PROPER BANGING VEGAN FOOD

MITCHELL BEAZLEY

First published in Great Britain in 2018 by Mitchell Beazley,
an imprint of Octopus Publishing Group Ltd
Carmelite House, 50 Victoria Embankment, London EC4Y 0DZ
www.octopusbooks.co.uk

Text copyright © One Tribe TV Limited 2018
Design and layout copyright © Octopus Publishing Group 2018
Creamy Mushroom Pie on page 124 © Mr Nice Pie, 2018
Pizza on page 136 © One Planet Pizza, 2018
Aquafaba Pavlovas on page 201 © Sara Williams, 2018

ISBN 978-1-78472-596-9

A CIP catalogue record for this book is available from the British Library.

Printed and bound in Italy

10 9 8 7 6 5 4 3 2 1

Editorial Director Eleanor Maxfield
Senior Editor Pauline Bache
Design and Art Direction Smith & Gilmour
Photographer (portraits) Chris Terry
Photographer (food) Jamie Orlando Smith
Food Stylist Phil Mundy
Props Stylist Olivia Wardle
Recipe Developer Rob Andrew
Cover Illustrator Andy Smith
Creative Director Jonathan Christie
Production Manager Caroline Alberti

CONTENTS

PRITCH'S PREFACE

I've written this book primarily with two types of readers in mind – those who are new to vegan cookery and are looking for simple ideas for some tasty grub, and also, anyone who might not be the most experienced cook and wants recipes that are easy to follow and a bit no-nonsense. Actually, there's a third type of reader I had in mind, too – the one who wants to eat really healthy food that's also seriously tasty!

If cooking seems to you to be something difficult and mysterious, I would really like to stress that, actually, making a delicious meal can be nothing more than a matter of going through a few simple steps. With stews and casseroles you just shove it all together and stick it in the oven. Chilli is the easiest – just whack it on the stove to simmer. With salads you're simply chopping stuff up. Just give it a go. Cookbooks can be really intimidating. I hope this one isn't.

If you're new to veganism, I've been there! When I went vegan I didn't know where to start. It seemed like another language sometimes, but after a month I discovered it wasn't so hard. After a few hangovers, once I realized there were plenty of fantastic vegan hangover foods, too, I knew I'd be OK!

This book is for anyone who wants to try vegan cooking or find new ways to eat vegan – whether you're dipping in a few meals a week, or going for it 100 per cent. This type of diet is definitely not just for athletes! With help from a top cook called Rob Andrew in Devon, I've filled this book with recipes that are easy to follow, and that I hope will show how uncomplicated vegan cooking can be. I've heard stories about people who went vegan, but switched back because they were becoming ill from not getting the right nutrients. At the end of the day your body is always needing vitamins and nutrients, as you are using them up constantly. You need to replenish them. My philosophy is to cram in as much as I possibly can into every meal and make it taste bangin'!

I'm still learning every day. This show has taught me a lot, which has been exciting. And this book is the cherry on the cake. I hope you all enjoy cooking from it as much as I have enjoyed putting it together.

PRITCHARD
Skateboarder, Triathlete, Cook

FROM STUNTMAN TO CHEF

As you dip into or cook your way through this book, you might wonder how someone who is so loud and out there on TV can be so different on paper, writing a vegan cookbook of all things! I guess I would explain it as I've always found happiness in the kitchen – it's where I chill out. The guy on TV is not who I am all the time.

I find it hard to sit still, so cooking gives me a way of slowing down a bit and focusing on something, without stopping completely. I love cooking – that's why I went to catering college – and for me it's a bit of a creative outlet too. I love how you can come up with a cracking bit of food to share or enjoy just for myself. Even if I'm properly hungover I'll get cooking – it just makes me feel better. I hope you'll find a similar sort of enjoyment in it too. So here's a bit of background on how I made the transformation from stuntman to chef...

STUNTMAN DREAMIN'

When I was at school I always wanted to be either a stuntman or a chef. You can picture the look on the career adviser's face when I told her I wanted to be a stuntman! Not the most realistic of plans, or even something that's considered a proper job. I put the stuntman idea to the back of my head, where it simmered away.

Cooking was always an interest. I loved food and my mother's cooking was always great. Like so many people, I learned by watching my mother. She would cook and we'd all sit round the table and eat, and that's how it was back then – a family unit around a table, talking and eating. People have busier lives now, and ready-prepped meals that take five minutes to microwave abound. Those family values, and the special encounters that take place around the table, seem to be fading into history, and I feel something important is lost in convenience.

THE COLLEGE YEARS

Thanks to my mother and the joys of cooking, I decided to be a chef and learn the ins and outs of the service and restaurant industry. As soon as I left school I went to Colchester Avenue Catering College in Cardiff (it's sadly not there anymore) to study for two great years, during which I was taught by some highly efficient army chefs! Our head teacher was a guy called Mr Reeves. They say you'll always remember a good teacher. We could banter and have a laugh, but when he was serious he really was serious. He was mainly Head of House in the restaurant and I remember him being very professional, especially when it came to looking after his guests. He always smiled, had impeccable manners and this general aura that would light up the table he was talking to. He was sharp-witted and a great joker. The customer was his number one and he always made sure they had a good time. It's those values that I liked about him and I reckon they influenced my path in life.

Silver service wasn't for me, though. I'm not a very good people person and that, combined with my shyness, wasn't a good combination really. However, being in the kitchen was exciting and fast-paced and I loved it. Those army chefs were just like Gordon Ramsay, shouting and swearing at any given moment. At college I found that I excelled in the pastry department and would put out some great puddings, along with good-quality sugar work, which I enjoyed a great deal. I can't imagine anyone who has seen my *Dirty Sanchez* antics can think of me knuckling down to a bit of sugar craft!

Throughout my time in college I would skateboard any time I could – to college and back, and around the college grounds during lunch breaks, to the amusement of my classmates. They'd go to the pub at lunch or after college, and I would go skateboarding instead. Back then, skateboarding wasn't taken seriously as it is now. To them, I was still a big kid... nothing much has changed, really.

FIRST (AND LAST) CHEFFING GIG

I left college to hit the big bad world and find a job that would hopefully send me on a culinary journey to the top of my game.

I started walking into restaurants all over Cardiff handing in my CV, hoping to get my first job. I didn't expect much, and was prepared to start from the bottom and work my way up.

One day I walked into a Persian restaurant and takeaway and met the manager of the place, who gave me a job working beside the head chef. It was hard work, but I'm not scared of that. However I was young, just 19, and I was scared stiff of the manager. To cut a long story short, he bullied me from day one up until the day he sacked me. It was a horrendous experience that ruined my confidence and my love for cooking.

FACTORY LIFE

I never wanted to go back into a kitchen again after that gig, so I found myself another job. I still loved to cook, but it was something I did for myself now. I had a friend who was a window cleaner who offered me a job cleaning windows five days a week, so I took him up on the offer and spent my days outside in the fresh air. It was a great job as I had plenty of time on my hands to pursue my passion for skateboarding. This was to be my life for many years – window cleaning all day and skateboarding whenever I could, until pressure from my parents to get a job with more security pushed me into accepting another offer (of a job that I could still do when it rained).

My mate Matthew Dyer offered me a job in a factory making heating elements for industry. I sat in a seat from 8am until

5pm cutting metal tubes all day long with a huge motorized saw. It was mind-numbing work, a job that wasn't for me, but it brought the money in and paid the bills. I had three years there, and although I hated the work itself, I had plenty of fun with the people working there. I made people laugh. I was the factory clown, just as I had been the school clown and the college clown, and I was cool with that role. I remember they were always entertained by my dress sense being 'way out there' compared with everyone else's. I still love dressing up!

SKATING GETS SERIOUS

One weekend I went to Radlands Plaza skatepark in Northampton to enter a competition. Little did I know how that day was to shape my future. I came first in my age group and was offered sponsorship by a distribution company called Faze 7. They sorted me out with a monthly package of skateboards, shoes and clothes. As you can imagine, I was stunned but pleased. It was like Christmas every month as these huge boxes of goodies turned up. I then turned pro for a new British company called Panic. I couldn't believe it – I was now starting to get paid to do something I've loved since I was 15. It had become my full-time job to wake up and skate all day and travel the world with my team. Those years were so much fun!

But like anything in life, I could slowly see it fading away as time went on. I needed a back-up plan – a job in the skate industry, as that's all I knew, really... skateboarding. A distribution company in Porthcawl

started to distribute Globe skate shoes and the boss of Double Overhead Distribution, Brad Hockridge, popped into City Surf (my local skate shop) and offered me a managerial role, which I accepted straight away. I was still a pro, still travelling and skateboarding, but this time I got to do it with a team that I picked to ride for Globe.

MTV CALLING

While I was working for Globe, myself and my mate Dainton started capturing our skate antics along with our off-skateboard pranks on video, until we amassed enough footage to put together a whole sequence, which was titled *Pritchard vs Dainton*. It was a video full of skateboarding, pranks and stupid stunts, along with some shocking scenes that I won't detail here. Myself and Dainton then spent the next six months promoting the video and it slowly became the most talked-about British skate video of all time. We released the tape and the sales went through the roof. One day, while sitting in my office at Globe, I got a phone call from Martha Delap, a talent scout from MTV, asking if we could go in for a meeting about doing a possible TV show.

To cut a long story short, after a few meetings we signed up with MTV and started filming *Dirty Sanchez*. I thought the show would be a one off, but it took off massively and became MTV's biggest ever show at the time. It went out to 64 countries and over 400 million people, then during the next decade or so I worked on three series of *Sanchez*, a *Sanchez* movie, a series of *Wrecked*, and a series of *Sanchez Gets High*, *Balls of Steel* and *Death Wish Live* for Channel 4, as well as an XFM radio show, and received two Pop Factory rock'n'roll excess awards. Life went from nought to sixty at a very quick pace, and with the success of the TV shows, live touring and non-stop parties, it all started to take its toll on my body.

A NEW FOCUS

It was time to make a serious life change and become fit again. The skateboarding had long gone, the TV shows and gigs were slowly drying up, my mental health was starting to suffer and I needed to find a new direction in life, and fast. I set myself a goal to run the Cardiff half marathon (I had done it at the age of 15) so began training. Very quickly I could feel myself getting an amazing fitness high from it – not the party type of high this time! I loved it. The day came and I completed the half marathon in 1 hour 45 minutes. From then until the present day I have continued to enter sporting and endurance events. I really enjoy pushing my body to its limits, so I went down the Ironman route. I finished my first full Ironman race in 2011 at Bolton and, since then, I've completed Double and Triple Ironman events, done 30 Half Ironman Distances in 30 days (a world record at the time), run from John O'Groats to Land's End in 30 days, cycled John O'Groats to Land's End in 7 days, run 30 half marathons in 30 days, and swum Lake Windemere and Ullswater in the Lake District.

BACK TO THE KITCHEN

With all this fitness going on, I started getting back into food, as one of the most important aspects of fitness and endurance sports is diet and nutrition. In the early stages I was getting my foods wrong and eating far too much sweet stuff to give me the energy I needed to fuel my body and get me over the line.

While doing a lot of research online looking at the diets of triathletes, I realized that many of them were vegan. At the time I had always pigeonholed vegans into the 'weak' category, with no idea that, if done right, a vegan diet can really help a body deal with the demands of sports, and support and nurture the general health and wellbeing of your body. I found this interesting. The more I read about it, the more it made sense. I then came across the documentary *Cowspiracy* – a film that inspired me to make huge life changes. I watched with awe. I couldn't believe what I was seeing and hearing, and I didn't know there was so much more to veganism than just not eating meat and dairy. I never realized the damage we do, the strain we put on our planet – our homes – because of the way that animals are farmed for human consumption. I couldn't believe the cruelty and the lack of compassion. I've been an animal lover all my life. I actually love many animals more than I do humans, and yet, I was eating them. I felt I was ignorant to have believed it was OK to eat a pig, cow, lamb, but not a dog. I'm so grateful to those documentary makers for opening my eyes to the reality of dairy farming. People

choose to be vegan for many reasons –
for me, at first it was for my own health.
But after watching that documentary, the
welfare of all animals became an important
reason for being a vegan.

FLIPPING THE VEGAN SWITCH

The next morning after watching the film,
I decided to go vegan – it suddenly seemed
the most natural choice. And with that
a whole new world of foods and cooking
methods opened up to me. Three years into
veganism, I still find the whole experience
really interesting. Exploring replacements
for eggs, milk, cheese and meat got me
back into cooking again, and rekindled
the passion I had when I left college. I was
discovering the world of vegan ingredients,
and how to use them in dishes. And I was
rediscovering the mighty vegetable,
elevated from humble sidekick to the star
of the show. Far from feeling weak, hungry,
undernourished and bored, I was feeling
strong, healthy, energized, and was loving
my experiences in the kitchen, both in
terms of cooking and eating.

I was on a smooth ride with this vegan-
cooking journey and I wanted to do something
with it. I had the idea to start my own
YouTube cooking show. The only thing
holding me back was my nerves. 'Can I do
it? It's been so long though! What if people
think it's rubbish? Can I speak to the camera
like I used to?' I had all these things going
through my mind and was finding excuses
not to do it. I decided instead to focus on
the positives in the idea – such as inspiring
a younger generation to cook and eat

healthily, and showing others that you
can do an Ironman event on a vegan diet.
I realized that I am living proof that a
vegan can do 30 Half Ironmans in 30 days.
Sharing how I managed to fuel my body's
endurance was the right path for me.

As cheesy (vegan cheesy – haha) as it
sounds, nothing ever grows in the comfort
zone, so I grabbed the bull by the horns
and shared my idea with two guys, Pete
Pickford and James Threlfall, who I'd filmed
with in the past, who loved the idea.
We made plans and, in 2017, we launched
Pritchard's Proper Vegan Cooking. Although
I was really nervous at first, I absolutely
loved being in front of the camera again.
The show was a hit with many, which was
so exciting and humbling. I was surrounded
by a great team, and many positives have
come from it.

It's thanks to that YouTube show that I'm
now here, writing this book to accompany
the BBC TV series. I honestly can't explain
how mental it is to write this. When I look
back at myself at catering college, I know
I would never have thought I'd be writing a
cookbook 25 years later! I don't call myself
a chef at all. I see myself as a cook – one that
likes cooking simple recipes that others
find easy to follow.

TOP INGREDIENTS, KIT & TIPS

TOP INGREDIENTS

There are some ingredients I never let myself run out of:

1. HIMALAYAN SALT

I was introduced to Himalayan salt at my local vegan restaurant, Anna Loka, in Cardiff. It's the purest you can get and is packed full of minerals. Tastes amazing – especially on tomatoes.

2. FRUIT

Brilliant in my morning smoothie. (Sometimes I add a shot of coffee too!) I use fruit a lot – particularly bananas and blueberries – when I do endurance events. My body is so knackered I can't eat, but a smoothie goes down, well, smoothly, and gives me all the carbs I need. Works a treat. Keep fruit in your freezer to always have some to hand. Be aware that pesticide use abounds in commercial fruit cultivation. I'm buying more organic fruit and veg as I know it's proper food, not alien stuff. It's a bit more expensive, but pay the extra if you can.

3. OAT MILK

Add it to smoothies or cereal, and it's the only plant-based milk that goes well with coffee and tea. (You shouldn't have too much soya – I've heard it gives you man boobs...)

4. BEANS/PULSES

I have canned and dried in my cupboard, always organic. In a rush, I use canned, but they are so much better dried and soaked – they have a meatier texture and more nutrients, in my opinion. Put them in stews, chillis and casseroles.

5. GARLIC

At least 4 cloves in a casserole.

6. TOMATOES

I love fresh salads in the summer – red onion, fresh basil, balsamic vinegar and thick slices of fragrant, sweet tomato on bread – just lush. Organic tomatoes have amazing flavour, so if you have some outdoor space, consider growing them in the summer and picking fresh every day.

7. PAPRIKA

Paprika, smoked paprika and dried chilli – the warming, flavourful products of pepper plants – are never out of stock in my kitchen. I love the smoky barbecue flavour of smoked paprika, but use it sparingly. I was once too enthusiastic and had to bin the whole dinner – tasted awful. Used wisely, it's deeply savoury and enriches the flavours of a dish nicely.

8. GARAM MASALA

I use this spice blend as my base for curries. Failsafe, when you use the right amount.

9. COCONUT OIL

I fry with this as it has a highish smoke point. I also add it to smoothies sometimes – I like the hint of coconut at the back of every mouthful.

10. OLIVE OIL

There are some things you're willing to put your hand in your pocket for, to ensure you get quality stuff. Olive oil is one of them. Buy light oil for cooking and spend extra on something for dressings and drizzling. (Balsamic vinegar is another thing that it's worth digging deeper for. Get the Modena stuff and one that is aged.)

11. SPAGHETTI HOOPS

Not an ingredient, but I always have a can in my cupboard as I love them and always will! Of course, they've got to be served on toast. And buy the cheap ones, the leading brand isn't actually vegan.

TOP KIT

You don't need fancy kit to produce top meals – just a knife, a chopping board and some good ingredients. But over time you might like to invest in a few gadgets that make things quicker and easier. This is my essential kit:

KITCHEN KNIFE

I use a huge chopping cleaver, suits me just fine for chopping veg, and the huge blade is handy for scooping chopped-up items from the board to shove into the saucepan.

WOK

I love my stir fries – I have one every week. Take minutes to throw together and so tasty.

ELECTRIC SPIRALIZER

Spiralized carrot salads and courgetti spaghetti are just the start. There is so much inspiration to help vegans make the most of a spiralizer – a quick internet search will give you oodles of ideas. The hand-crank variety is fine, but an electric spiralizer makes things so much faster. If you don't have one, just use a vegetable peeler to cut your veg into fine ribbons instead, and use ribbons of veg in raw dishes and salads. (Apart from peeling potatoes, this is the only use my peeler ever gets – I try to keep skins on as much as possible.)

FOOD PROCESSOR AND/OR HIGH-POWERED BLENDER

I use one or both of these every day. A food processor can be your chopping slave if you have a mountain of slicing to do, and makes quick and easy work of whisking, kneading and beating. A blender, especially a high-powered one (like the NutriBullet) is great for making smoothies and nut milks, blending soups, and releasing stubborn beasts from inside their husks, also great for grinding chia, flax and pumpkin seeds.

VEGAN BEWARE!

There can be animal products lurking in the most innocuous places. Here are a few things that I've learned along the way:

Lots of beers and wines aren't vegan so check the bottle first. However there are some great vegan wines. And while we're on drinks, some brands of orange juice can include fish oil – yuk!

Look out for gelatine in a lot of jelly sweets and desserts.

You'll be surprised how many things have milk in where you wouldn't even expect it so check the ingredients.

In fact, it's always wise to check the ingredients of any ready-prepared, packaged food, including breads and condiments. Worcestershire sauce has anchovies in it for example, and naan breads traditionally include dairy yogurt.

Best thing that I discovered was vegan…? Hobnobs, nom nom.

Finally, get ready for non-vegans giving you masses of abuse and surround yourself with animals for a happy peaceful life.

MORNING KICK-START

These are my go-to things to eat in the morning after coming out of the gym or pool, off the bike, or back from my run. I try to put as much into my system in the morning as I can, as sometimes I miss lunch. When I've got a lot of time on my hands I don't stop freakin' eating.

PREP: 5 MINUTES ★ COOK: 20–30 MINUTES

BEETROOT JUICE PANCAKES

MAKES 16

350g porridge oats
250ml plant-based milk
   (I use oat milk)
250ml beetroot juice
2 bananas
1 teaspoon baking powder
coconut oil, for frying

To serve
blueberries, strawberries
   or any fruit of your choice
oat cream
maple syrup

Beetroot has been proven to boost stamina. It's my go-to natural steroid – I'll drink a litre of beetroot juice the day before a competition. I normally make these light, delicious pancakes during the week as a treat to give me that much-needed burst of energy. Try them topped with fresh fruit.

I make the batter for these pancakes in a blender. Put the oats into your blender and blitz to a flour-like consistency. Now add the milk and the beetroot juice and blend, then add the bananas and baking powder and blitz again until the mixture resembles pancake batter.

Put a frying pan on your hob over medium heat and melt 1 teaspoon coconut oil in it. Scoop 1 tablespoon batter into the pan for each pancake and cook for about 2½ minutes on the first side, until slightly golden. Flip over and cook for a further 2 minutes on the second side in the same way. Once cooked, transfer to a plate and keep warm in a low oven while you make the remaining pancakes in the same way. Keep adding them to the plate and stack 'em high.

Add your fave fruit, drizzle with oat cream and maple syrup and hoover them bad boys up. Then grab yer bike and smash some miles.

HANGOVER SMOOTHIE and LAVERBREAD 'OYSTERS'

SERVES 4

4 ice-cold shots of vodka
(optional)

For the smoothie
2 celery sticks
600ml tomato juice
1 avocado
½ cucumber
4 big green olives (optional)
1 tablespoon freshly grated
horseradish (or use ginger)
1 tablespoon vegan
Worcestershire sauce
6 ice cubes
few grinds of black pepper
sriracha hot sauce, to taste
celery salt, to taste
lemon juice, to taste

For the 'oysters'
80g laverbread
red wine vinegar, to sprinkle
1 small shallot, finely diced

This is my version of Bloody Mary and oysters. The vodka is, of course, optional. Laverbread is a particularly Welsh delicacy of seaweed cooked down into a dark green purée. It is as close to seafood as a vegan will get, with its deep, salty, mineral flavour. Some people find it a bit too much, but to me it's the goodness of the sea on a spoon. You can buy it fresh or canned. Either shoot back your 'oyster' fast or chew and savour it – the choice is yours.

Cut 1 of the celery sticks into 4 long batons, to act as stirrers, and set aside. Cut the other into rough pieces and add to a blender with the tomato juice, avocado, cucumber, olives, horseradish, Worcestershire sauce, ice cubes and pepper. Whizz until smooth. Add a dash of water if the smoothie seems too thick. Taste the mixture and tweak the flavour to your liking with sriracha, celery salt and a squeeze or 2 of lemon juice. Keep chilled until needed.

For the 'oysters', choose 4 large spoons (ramen spoons are best, if you have any) and place a 20-g dollop of laverbread on each spoon. Give each a small shake of vinegar and top with a little of the chopped shallot.

Divide the smoothie between 4 glasses and garnish each with a celery stick baton. Rack up 4 ice-cold shots of vodka, if you like.

Shoot the 'oysters' in one, giving them a quick chew as you do. Knock back the vodka and then relax and tuck into the smoothie at your leisure.

★ ✦ ★ TOFU ★ ✦ ★
SCRAMBLED EGGS

SERVES 2

2 tablespoons olive oil or
    coconut oil
½ red onion, finely sliced
4 broccoli florets, finely chopped
225g extra-firm tofu
½ teaspoon Himalayan salt
½ teaspoon garlic powder
½ teaspoon turmeric
½ teaspoon chilli flakes,
    or to taste
¼ teaspoon smoked paprika

To serve
toast
Smoky Baked Beans
    (see page 27)

This is usually a weekend morning treat. It's basically the same idea as scrambled eggs though – and I know it sounds odd – add turmeric for flavour and colour. Depending on what tofu you use, it can be very silky and moist. It doesn't taste like egg, but is just as satisfying. Use it as part of your Full Hangover Pile Up breakfast (see page 25), or just have it on toast with baked beans.

Heat the oil in a frying pan. Put the onion and broccoli into the warmed oil in the frying pan and gently fry over medium-low heat for 2–3 minutes, until they are cooked but still have a little crunch in them.

Grab the tofu and either scramble it with a fork or cut it into bite-sized pieces. Add it to the pan and stir well. Now add the salt, spices and a splash of water if it looks too thick or dry. Cook for 2 minutes, until the tofu is heated through. Serve on toast with some baked beans.

THE FULL HANGOVER PILE UP

SERVES 4

I've made an art form of the vegan full breakfast. This will help you heal from last night's antics and fuel you for today's mischief. Serve any of the individual elements alone for a light breakfast, but put them all together for the full-on curative effect. Integral to the pile up are sliced Seitan English Breakfast Sausage (see page 145) and Tofu Scrambled Eggs (see page 22), so don't forget to add those to the table alongside the three recipes below. Serve the whole lot with hot toast and strong tea. Thankfully ketchup and HP sauce are vegan. Unless you are god-like in your multitasking-while-hungover skills, I suggest you make the seitan and beans ahead of time, and it's even worth boiling the spuds in advance, too – you'll still have a bit of work to do for someone who's worse for wear. Cross your fingers that someone else offers to wash up.

PREP: 5 MINUTES ★ COOK: 20 MINUTES

GARLIC MUSHROOMS
★

olive oil, for greasing
2 garlic cloves, crushed
75g soft vegan spread
lemon juice, to taste
4 Portobello mushrooms
salt and pepper

Bake these in the oven on the shelf below the smashed potato cakes (see page 26). Use olive oil if you can't find a good vegan spread.

Preheat the oven to 200°C (Gas Mark 6). Grease a roasting tray with oil.

Mix the garlic with the vegan spread and a good squeeze of lemon juice in a bowl.

Arrange the mushrooms with their stalk sides facing up in the prepared roasting tray. Divide the flavoured spread between the mushrooms and smear the mixture into the gills. Season with salt and pepper.

Pop the mushrooms into the oven and roast for 20 minutes, until cooked through.

SMASHED POTATO CAKES
★

12 small new potatoes
olive oil
about 4 sprigs of thyme,
  leaves picked, to taste
salt and pepper

Quicker than bubble and squeak, less faff than a hash brown, these are just squashed and roasted potatoes but, somehow, they seem like so much more. They are best made with new or salad potatoes.

Boil the potatoes, whole and with their skins on, in plenty of salted water for about 10–12 minutes until just tender. Drain well. (This can be done well in advance as they can be cooked from cold later on. Keep them in the fridge until you're ready to use them.)

Preheat the oven to 200°C (Gas Mark 6). Line a roasting tray with baking paper, brush it liberally with olive oil and scatter over some salt.

Evenly space the potatoes in the prepared tray, then press each potato down so that it flattens but stays in 1 piece. I use the flat side of my cleaver, but you could use the bottom of a mug, a potato masher or the flat of your hand (if cooking the potatoes from cold). Brush the flattened spuds with plenty of oil and season with salt. Roast for 25 minutes, then remove the tray from the oven and scatter over some fresh thyme leaves and grind over some black pepper. Return the tray to the oven for a final 10 minutes, or until the potatoes are golden and crisp. Serve immediately.

Pictured on page 24

SMOKY BAKED BEANS

★

1 red onion, sliced
olive oil
1 tablespoon tomato purée
500g passata
1 tablespoon balsamic vinegar
2 teaspoons sweet smoked
    paprika
1 bay leaf
2 teaspoons brown sugar
400g can haricot beans
salt and pepper

These are easily made in advance. Blending some of the beans and sauce gives the whole thing a more Heinzy texture.

Heat a little oil in a saucepan. Add the onion and fry over medium-low heat for 10 minutes, until starting to soften.

Add the tomato purée, passata, vinegar, paprika, bay leaf and sugar to the pan. Season with salt and pepper. Bring up to a simmer and cook gently for 10 minutes.

Stir the haricot beans into the saucepan and cook for a further 10 minutes, until the sauce has thickened.

When ready, you have the option to transfer a quarter of the beans to a blender and whizz them up until smooth, then return the blended beans to the pan and stir through before serving.

Pictured on page 24

BIRCHER OVERNIGHT OATS

SERVES 2

2 apples, grated
150g oats
pinch of cinnamon
2 teaspoons brown sugar
400ml almond milk,
    plus extra to finish
2 teaspoons lemon juice

Optional additions
dried fruit – sultanas, raisins,
    chopped figs, apricots,
    cranberries or dehydrated
    raspberries and strawberries
seeds – chia, flax, sunflower,
    sunflower or pumpkin
nuts – flaked almonds, chopped
    hazelnuts, cashews,
    pecans or Brazils
1 tablespoon cacao powder
flaked coconut

Suggested toppings
fresh fruit of any ilk – berries
    in particular, but sliced mango,
    pineapples, bananas and
    papaya work well, too
toasted nuts or seeds
jam, compote or stewed fruit
nut butters
a blob of vegan yogurt
dates, soaked in hot tea
a double shot of espresso coffee
finely chopped stem ginger
    and plenty of the syrup
maple syrup

Most muesli is better if it has time to soak up the milk a little. I think it's even better if soaked overnight – no more powdery oats. They plump up and soften nicely during the soak, meaning breakfast can be pulled, fully formed, from the fridge in the morning. You can add a little extra milk before serving, depending on your preferred consistency – it's a matter of personal taste. And you can add any number of delicious ingredients to the muesli to make it even more your own. I give a few suggestions below, but feel free to go your own way.

Mix the apple, oats, cinnamon, sugar, milk and lemon juice in a bowl. You might like to mix in as much or as little as any of the suggested optional additions.

Cover the bowl, transfer it to the fridge and leave overnight.

In the morning, give the mixture a quick mix and add a little extra milk if it seems a little too thick. Divide it among 2 serving bowls. Serve it as is, or with a topping of your choice.

PRITCH'S PORRIDGE
SERVES 1

The perfect winter breakfast. Below is my basic formula for a generous bowl of porridge. The purist would insist on adding nothing more than water and salt to the oats. I say forget that! Live a little. So I'm offering a few recipe variations that inject a bit of colour and extra flavour to brighten up your day. I use good old fashioned oats, but nowadays people like to add seeds and grains such as chia, quinoa, rye, barley or amaranth, to add some protein. Try mixing one or more of these, 50/50 with the oats. Bear in mind that the cooking time and the amount of liquid you need may increase.

THE BASIC FORMULA
★

If you prefer things simple, you need go no further than this – creamy and satisfying.

50g porridge oats
250ml almond milk, plus extra as desired
small pinch of sea salt

Place the oats and milk in a saucepan and bring to a gentle simmer. Cook gently over medium-low heat for 10 minutes, stirring often. Finish with a pinch of salt stirred through. Add more milk to thin the porridge, if you like.

THE MARATHON BAR
★

This version is a bit more of a treat, but ideal if you're planning on burning some carbs first thing.

50g porridge oats
250ml almond milk, plus extra as desired
2 teaspoons light brown sugar
1 tablespoon cacao powder
2 tablespoons crunchy peanut butter
peanut halves, to serve

Cook as described opposite, stirring the sugar, cacao and peanut butter in at the end and omitting the salt. Serve scattered with peanut halves.

MARMALADE, TOAST and TEA

★

....

Yep, in porridge. Sounds nutty but works. Keep a close eye on the bread when you put it in the oven to brown, as it can burn easily. This is one for when you've a bit more time to cook brekkie!

....

50g coconut oil
2 slices of day-old sourdough bread, crusts
    removed and bread torn into 2cm pieces
40g caster sugar
250ml almond milk, plus extra as desired
1 English Breakfast teabag
50g porridge oats
small pinch of sea salt
marmalade, to top

Preheat the oven to 180°C (Gas Mark 4).

Melt the oil in a frying pan over medium-low heat. Stir in the sugar and, once it has dissolved in the hot oil, add the torn bread pieces. Turn them well so they soak up as much of the sweetened oil as they can.

Transfer the bread pieces to a baking tray and bake for 12–15 minutes, turning occasionally, until golden brown and crunchy. (This may take longer, depending on the freshness of the bread.) Remove from the oven and allow to cool. These will keep well for 3–4 days in an airtight container, or for 3–4 months in the freezer.

Heat the almond milk in a saucepan over medium heat until it is just beginning to boil. Take the pan off the heat and add the teabag. Leave to brew for 5 minutes. Remove the teabag, stir in the oats and cook as described on page 31. Serve topped with a blob of marmalade and the crispy toast.

Pictured on page 30

BANANA and BERRIES

★

....

Cooking the blueberries brings a jammy-like feel to this brekkie. Perks you right up.

....

handful of blueberries
1 banana, sliced
250ml almond milk, plus extra as desired
50g porridge oats
small pinch of sea salt
handful of raspberries
handful of strawberries

Place the blueberries in a saucepan over medium-low heat and heat for 3–4 minutes, until they begin to soften and burst. Slice in the banana and mash it into the blueberries with a fork. Add the milk and oats and cook as described on page 31. Serve topped with the fresh berries.

Pictured on page 30

BLUEBERRY DROP SCONE PANCAKES

MAKES 10–12

For the fruit
100g blueberries
1 tablespoon brown sugar
squeeze of lime juice

For the pancakes
100ml aquafaba (the liquid
   from a can of chickpeas)
200g plain or wholemeal flour
1 tablespoon baking powder
30g caster sugar
1 tablespoon vegetable oil,
   plus extra for frying
250ml almond milk
1 tablespoon cider vinegar
small pinch of salt

To serve (optional)
vegan yogurt
maple syrup

This recipe uses a bit of vegan magic: aquafaba. You can make the pancakes without it, but they won't come out nearly as light and fluffy.

Cook the blueberries in a small saucepan with the sugar and lime juice for 3–4 minutes, until they start to burst and release a little juice. Remove from the heat and set aside.

Put the aquafaba into a clean bowl and use a handheld electric whisk or stick blender to whisk for about 5 minutes, until it is light, fluffy and forms firm peaks.

Sift the flour and baking powder into a mixing bowl. Add the sugar, oil, milk, vinegar and a small pinch of salt. Whisk together until smooth.

Fold the aquafaba into the batter as gently as you can, ensuring it is thoroughly mixed in. Ripple the blueberries through the mixture.

Heat a layer of oil in a nonstick frying pan. Dollop generous spoonfuls of batter into the pan. Cook over medium heat for 3–4 minutes, until golden brown on the bottom. Flip over and cook the other side for 2–3 minutes, until golden brown. If you don't have a wide enough frying pan, you'll need to cook these in 2 batches, so keep the first lot warm in a low oven while you cook the second batch.

Serve warm, topped with your favourite yogurt and maybe a drizzle of maple syrup.

GRANOLA

MAKES 1.5KG

450g jumbo oats
250g mixed seeds
250g almonds
100g light brown sugar
1 teaspoon ground cinnamon
½ teaspoon ground ginger
½ teaspoon sea salt
160ml maple syrup
2 tablespoons sunflower oil
125g dried apricots, chopped
125g dried figs, chopped
125g pitted dates, chopped

This recipe is EXTREMELY ADAPTABLE! Add more salt or spice to suit your taste, and change the nuts or fruit to your preference. You may not use this granola every day, but it's simple to make, it keeps well if stored right, and it gives you an easy go-to option on a busy day.

Preheat the oven to 170˚C (Gas Mark 3½).

Put all the ingredients, except the chopped dried fruit, into a bowl and mix them together thoroughly. Spread out the mixture evenly across 2 large baking trays.

Bake for 40–50 minutes, turning every 10 minutes, until golden and crunchy. Bear in mind that the top tray may cook more quickly than the lower one.

Allow to cool on the baking tray slightly, then mix in the dried fruits. Leave to cool completely. Store in an airtight container for up to a month.

NUT MILK

SERVES 1

150g blanched nuts of
your choice
2 dates, pitted and chopped
(optional for a sweet milk)
1 teaspoon vanilla extract
(optional for a sweet milk)

Almond, hazelnut, cashews – the choice is yours. Find a health food shop that sells them loose as supermarket nuts are hugely overpriced. The more you buy, the more cost effective the whole exercise becomes. This is a really handy recipe to have, because there are many uses for nut milk – smoothies, cereals, when you fancy a vegan white Russian as a nightcap... And there is another bonus – you can use the byproduct pulp for making the delicious Energy Balls on page 42.

Put the nuts into a bowl of water and leave to soak overnight. They will swell up as they absorb water.

Next day, drain the water and rinse the nuts. Put them into a high-powered blender (I use my NutriBullet) and add roughly 300ml of water. Throw in the dates and add the vanilla extract if using. Blend for approximately 3 minutes in 1-minute bursts, until everything is pulped up.

Line a sieve with a muslin cloth. Set this over a bowl or saucepan. Tip the blitzed mixture into the cloth-lined sieve. Leave the mixture to strain for 10 minutes, then tightly squeeze to ensure all the milk has strained out.

Transfer the pulp left in the muslin cloth to an airtight container and store in the fridge or freezer, to use for making energy balls. Decant the strained nut milk into a sealable jar and store it in the fridge for up to 4 days.

SMACK-YOU-IN-THE-FACE SMOOTHIE

SERVES 1

1 banana
5 strawberries
handful of spinach
150ml apple juice
ice, to taste

I like to start my day with this: easy to make, easy to drink and gives you a quick slap in the face to get you kicking and wake you up. Consider this a starting point – you can add whatever you want for the nutrients and flavours your body is asking for. This is a great one for pouring into your protein shaker beaker to take out with you to work or the gym.

Whack all the ingredients into the bowl of a food processor and blitz until smooth. Pour the mixture straight into a glass to serve.

★ PREP: 5 MINUTES ★

BREAKFAST JUICE

SERVES 1

50g watercress
1 tablespoon flaxseed oil
200ml orange juice
ice, to taste

You really can do anything with this – or whack anything in – try it. I put tofu or coconut oil in mine sometimes to give it an extra rich, creamy hit. This is crammed with good stuff.

Put the watercress and flaxseed oil into a blender and blitz until liquid. Pour in the orange juice. Blend again for 30 seconds. Pour straight into a glass to serve.

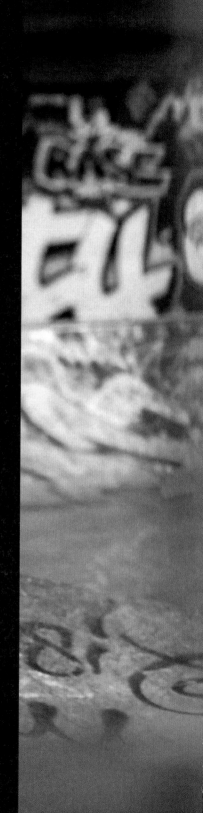

I turn to these when I'm in a hurry or need a bit more after dinner. I'll often miss lunch, so these keep me going.

ENERGY BALLS

MAKES 12

4 dates, pitted
50g cashew nuts
½ teaspoon vanilla extract
50g Huel (available from
Huel.com – or use oats,
ground to a flour in a
high-powered blender)
75g crunchy peanut butter
2 tablespoons agave nectar
1 tablespoon coconut oil
50g almond pulp (see page 36) or
2 tablespoons ground almond,
plus extra as required
chia seeds, desiccated coconut
or raw cacao powder,
for coating

I reach for one of these whenever I need an instant boost of energy, like when I'm cycling. Keep them in your back pocket and they provide the nudge you need to get to the next post – and beyond. They also make a great snack to take to work to get you through the day,

Put the dates, cashew nuts, vanilla extract, Huel or ground oats, peanut butter, agave nectar and coconut oil into a high-powered blender (I use a NutriBullet). Add a handful of almond pulp to the mixture. Turn on the blender and blitz. You might find the mixture sticks to the sides, so give the blender a shake. The mixture needs to be dry enough to hold together, but moist enough for you to roll into balls. If necessary, add more almond pulp to adjust the moistness of the mixture.

Spread out your chosen coating in a shallow dish. Line a tray with baking paper.

Divide the mixture into 12 portions. Roll these into balls in the palms of your hands, then roll each ball into your coating of choice and set it on the prepared tray. Transfer to the fridge and leave to firm up and set for about 2 hours. Then plonk 1 in your mouth and dance like Beyoncé for the day.

(CRAFT) BEER-BATTERED SUMMER VEG WITH AIOLI

SERVES 2

For the aioli
150ml Vegan Mayo
    (see page 175)
1 garlic clove, crushed

For the veg
sunflower or vegetable oil,
    for deep-frying
selection of fresh summer
    veg, about 700g in total
    (we used ½ a red pepper,
    sliced lengthways,
    ½ a courgette, sliced in
    half-moons, 500g green
    beans, trimmed, and
    ½ a small fennel)
lemon wedges, to serve

For the batter
90ml sparkling pale ale, chilled
25g plain flour
25g rice flour (or another
    25g plain flour)
½ tablespoon cornflour
½ tablespoon bicarbonate
    of soda
good pinch of salt

Join the craft beer revolution in style. With this dish the trick is to mix the batter just before use, so make sure you have everything ready to go. These fritters are best eaten immediately with a cold glass of the beer you used for the batter.

To make the aioli, mix the crushed garlic clove into the vegan mayo. Set aside in the fridge.

Pour approximately 4cm oil into a high-sided saucepan that is wide enough to fit the longer stems of your trimmed veggies. Slowly bring the oil up to 190°C over medium heat.

While the oil heats up, make the batter. Mix the beer with the flours, bicarb and a good pinch of salt in a bowl, working fast and loose (give it a stir rather than a whisk, as you want a few lumps and imperfections).

Dip a few pieces of veg into the batter and carefully lower them into the hot oil. Don't fry more than 6 pieces at a time or else the oil temperature will drop too much. Fry for 2 minutes or so, until golden, crisp and buoyant. Remove carefully with a slotted spoon and drain on a plate lined with kitchen paper. Dip and fry the remaining pieces of veg in the same way in batches.

Serve with lemon wedges and the aioli and dip and scoff while they are hot!

CHICKPEA KICKSHAWS WITH COCONUT SAMBAL

MAKES 16

For the kickshaws
olive oil, for frying
1 red onion, sliced
pinch of salt
1 garlic clove, crushed
2 tomatoes, roughly chopped
400g can chickpeas (reserve
    the liquid to use as aquafaba
    in other recipes)
¼ teaspoon chilli flakes
1 teaspoon cumin seeds
1 teaspoon turmeric
2 teaspoons garam masala
150g baby spinach
500g block of vegan puff pastry
½ tablespoon Dijon mustard
1 teaspoon black onion seeds
pepper

For the sambal
4 tablespoons desiccated
    coconut
1 spring onion, chopped
1 garlic clove, crushed
1 green chilli, chopped
1 large bunch of coriander
1 tablespoon olive oil,
    plus extra as required
salt

Kickshaws are tasty deep-fried pastry titbits, not too dissimilar to samosas. I've forgone the deep-fryer for an oven instead, but the essence is still there. Note that the cooler the filling mixture is, the easier it is to handle the pastry, so leave it to cool for as long as you can. Ideally, make the filling the day before and let it chill overnight in the fridge.

Heat a little olive oil in a saucepan over medium-low heat. Add the onion and a pinch of salt and cook gently for 10 minutes, until softened. Stir in the garlic, tomatoes, chickpeas and spices and cook gently for another 10 minutes, until most of the liquid has disappeared. Now mix in the spinach and cook until just wilted. Use a fork to mash the chickpeas until partially broken up. Season to taste, then remove from the heat and chill in the fridge.

Roll out the pastry to a thickness of 3–4mm. Cut it into 16 equal squares.

When the filling is cool, preheat your oven to 200°C (Gas Mark 6). Line a baking tray with baking paper.

Place a generous tablespoon of the filling mixture on the centre of 1 square of pastry. Brush the pastry edges with a little water, then fold 1 corner of the square over the filling to the diagonally opposite corner to conceal

Recipe continued overleaf

Recipe continued

the filling and create a triangle shape. Press the pastry edges together to seal the parcel. Repeat with the remaining pastry squares and filling. Arrange the pastry parcels on the prepared baking tray.

Put the mustard into a bowl with 1 tablespoon oil and whisk together. Brush the kickshaws with the mustard mixture, then sprinkle over the black onion seeds. Bake for 20 minutes, until golden.

While the kickshaws are baking, make the relish. Put the coconut into a mug and pour over enough boiling water to just cover. Leave to steep for 10 minutes. Drain away any excess water and place the coconut into a small food processor with the spring onion, garlic, chilli, coriander and oil. Blitz to a coarse paste, almost like pesto, adding a dash more oil if it seems dry. (Alternatively, smash it all together using a pestle and mortar, or finely chop everything and mix it together.) Season with salt.

Serve the kickshaws hot or cold with the sambal alongside for dipping.

TOMATO BRUSCHETTA

SERVES 2

approximately 6 ripe tomatoes,
cut into bite-sized chunks
½ red onion, finely diced
bunch of basil, chopped,
stalks and all
¼–½ green chilli (depending
on how hot you like it!),
deseeded if preferred
1 garlic clove, finely chopped
3 tablespoons good-quality
olive oil
3 tablespoons good-quality
balsamic vinegar
2 slices of good-quality bread
vegan butter
salt and pepper

This dish never fails to put a smile on my face. The smells and colours always remind me of happy summer days. Use plenty of ripe tomatoes of any type to make this – the more, the merrier. Save the other half of the avocado used here by leaving the stone in, putting it into an airtight container and keeping it in the fridge. It will last longer that way. This is good for snacking, a light lunch, or to start you off before you move on to dinner!

Put the tomatoes into a roomy bowl. Add the red onion, basil, chilli and garlic and mix well, then mix in the olive oil and balsamic vinegar. Season generously with salt and pepper (I love Himalayan salt – it's full of extra minerals and brilliant for replacing salts for the athletes among you). Gently stir the mixture, then leave it to stand for a while to allow the flavours to mix and mingle. About 10 minutes should do it.

Toast 2 nice chunky slices of bread. Put them onto serving plates, spread with dairy-free butter and pile on the good stuff – be generous. Eat straight away.

AVOCADO, TOMATO and MUSHROOM BRUSCHETTA

SERVES 2

handful of pine nuts
3 ripe tomatoes, cut into
    medium dice (or a good handful
    of bite-sized tomatoes)
olive oil, for drizzling
coconut oil
6 chestnut mushrooms, sliced
2 slices of tiger bread
1 garlic clove, halved
flesh of 1 large avocado
    (or 2 small), mashed with
    lemon juice to taste
sea salt and pepper
handful of basil leaves,
    chopped, to garnish

Three of my fave foods, served in an indecently enjoyable combination on top of a nice slab of toast. For me, it's got to be Tiger bread, but use the bread of your choice. This bruschetta is the ideal snack, but it also makes a good light lunch or a nutritious breakfast.

Toast the pine nuts in a dry frying pan over low heat for 2 minutes, until slightly brown. Set aside.

Put the tomato into a bowl and drizzle with a little olive oil, then season with salt and pepper and mix gently. Set aside.

Melt a little coconut oil in a frying pan. Add your mushrooms and fry over medium heat, stirring often, for about 5 minutes, until cooked through and tasty looking. Season with salt and pepper.

Meanwhile, toast your slices of tiger bread. As soon as they come out of the toaster, rub them with the halved garlic clove so they take on its flavour. Drizzle the toast with a little olive oil (or use a dairy-free spread if you wish) and put the slices on serving plates.

Grab the mashed avocado flesh and spread it onto the slices of toast, then top with the fried mushrooms and diced tomatoes. Sprinkle with the toasted pine nuts, garnish with chopped basil and enjoy straight away.

SUSHI SARNIES (ONIGIRAZU)

MAKES 6

For the sushi sarnies
400g firm marinated tofu
sunflower or vegetable oil,
    for frying
4 nori sheets
250g sushi rice, cooked to packet
    instructions and cooled
your chosen filling (see
    opposite for suggestions)

To serve
wasabi
soy sauce

These are like the brutish big brother of a Californian roll. Rice and tasty stuff, wrapped in seaweed. There is less faff and fiddle than with making sushi as you don't have to try to roll them like a perfect cigar. Marinated tofu is easy to buy in most supermarkets, but if you can't find it, just marinate some plain tofu in a little soy, tamari or teriyaki sauce overnight. Beyond the nori, rice and tofu, the world is your oyster (mushroom) in terms of filling. But I like to be helpful, so I've added a few suggestions below.

Slice the tofu into 4 even, flat rectangles. Heat the oil in a frying pan over a medium heat. Add the tofu rectangles and cook until golden on each side. Transfer the tofu to a plate and leave to cool.

Lay out a sheet of clingfilm and sit 1 nori sheet on the centre of it with the glossy side facing down. Place a rough rectangle (about the same size as your tofu rectangles) of sushi rice on the centre of the nori sheet. Push down on it gently to compress it as much as you can. On top of this, arrange a generous amount of your chosen filling (see below for ideas) and top with a tofu rectangle. Cover the tofu with some more sushi rice. It can be difficult to compress the final layer of rice without dislodging the layers beneath, so it helps to pack it on top of the tofu layer first, then add them both together.

Wet the edges of the nori sheet. Bring the corners into the middle to make a diamond shape. Then gather the clingfilm together and twist it to tighten the whole thing into a bun shape. Leave wrapped until ready to serve. Repeat with the remaining nori sheets, rice, filling and tofu.

To serve, cut each 'sarnie' in half to reveal the cross section of filling. Remove the clingfilm. Dip into wasabi-laced soy or tamari between bites.

Ideas for fillings:

BEETROOT, GINGER, PEAR AND SPINACH

Grate some raw beetroot. Shred some pickled sushi ginger and cut some under-ripe pear into matchsticks. Mix them together in a bowl with a pinch of salt and a little rice vinegar. Pack into the sushi sarnies and top with some fresh baby spinach leaves.

AVO AND SPRING VEG

Finely slice some radishes, spring onions and a few little gem lettuce leaves. Mix a blob of wasabi with a little rice vinegar and salt and dress the veg with this mixture. Stone, peel and slice an avocado. Fan it out on top of the sushi rice and top it with the wasbi-dressed veg.

CUCUMBER, CARROT AND SESAME

Use a vegetable peeler to slice some carrot and cucumber into thin strips. Mix these with a small handful of colourful bean sprouts, some freshly chopped red chilli and a scattering of black sesame seeds. Dress with a little rice vinegar and salt before packing into your sarnie.

TERIYAKI MUSHROOMS AND GREEN BEANS

Thinly slice and fry some oyster or shiitake mushrooms. Finish them with some chopped garlic and a dash of teriyaki sauce. Leave to cool before layering them into your sushi sandwich, alongside some lightly steamed green beans.

Pictured overleaf

SQUASH and SHROOM MOMOS WITH YUZU DIP

MAKES 20

For the momos
2 tablespoons vegetable or
    sunflower oil, plus extra
    for frying the momos
200g chestnut mushrooms,
    finely chopped
pinch of salt, plus extra to taste
400g peeled and grated squash
2 tablespoons vegan Thai red
    curry paste
small bunch of coriander,
    chopped
3 spring onions, finely chopped
20 egg-free Japanese dumpling
    wrappers/gyoza skins

For the dipping sauce
2 tablespoons yuzu
3 tablespoons soy sauce

If you try this dish, be prepared to feel the urgent need to make another batch immediately! Momos are the Tibetan answer to gyozas. In Nepal they are often served steamed, but I like to fry mine as well. This squash and mushroom filling is delicious and seriously moreish, and the yuzu dipping sauce enhances it very nicely. If you can't find yuzu, simply use lime juice instead.

Heat the oil in a frying pan. Add the mushrooms and salt and fry over high heat for 2–3 minutes, until the mushrooms begin to release their moisture. Add the squash and cook for a further 6 minutes or so, until the squash is slightly softened and the mix isn't too wet. Add the Thai paste, cook for 1 minute more, then remove from the heat. Stir in the coriander and onion. Taste and tweak the seasoning.

Place 1 tablespoon of the filling in the centre of a dumpling wrapper. Wet the edge of the wrapper and fold it over the filling to create a semicircle. Crimp the edges to seal. Repeat with the remaining wrappers and filling.

Transfer the dumplings to a steamer basket and steam for 5 minutes, in batches, until tender. While the momos steam, mix the yuzu with the soy in a bowl to make the dip.

Clean the frying pan and, when the momos have all been steamed, heat 2 tablespoons oil over medium heat. Fry the momos for 3–4 minutes, until the undersides are golden and crisp. Serve at once with the dipping sauce.

⚡ BABAGANOUSH WITH FLATBREADS ⚡

SERVES 4

For the babaganoush
2 large aubergines
olive oil
1 garlic clove, crushed
2 tablespoons tahini
1½ teaspoons ground cumin
3 tablespoons lemon juice
light brown muscovado
    sugar, to taste
salt

For the flatbreads
175g white bread flour,
    plus extra for dusting
125g wholemeal bread flour
1 tablespoon olive oil
½ teaspoon fine salt
175ml warm water

As good a dish to eat as it is a word to say. Babaganoush is usually used as a dip, or as part of a mezze alongside the hummus on page 172 and some fat green olives. If you can imagine yourself sipping mint tea in the shade, you're on the right track. Try tucking some into the kebab on page 120, or adding a slick of it into the burger on page 148.

Preheat a grill on a medium setting or light a barbecue. It has to be noted that cooking the aubergine will create some smoke, so the barbecue, or a well-ventilated kitchen, are ideal.

Rub the aubergines with oil. (Leave the green calyx attached at the top of each aubergine – it will hold everything together and provides a handle to hold when you're peeling them.) Put the aubergines under the grill or directly on the bars of a barbecue. Keep turning them every few minutes so they cook evenly. The idea here is to cook the aubergines whole until their skins are burnt and split, and the flesh is soft and collapsing. This should take about 20 minutes, depending on their sizes. They are ready when they feel perfectly soft. Check this by squeezing them with a pair of tongs, not your fingers – they love to belch scalding steam from their bellies when prodded. (If you don't have a grill or access to a barbecue, you can ape this method by roasting the aubergines whole in an oven at 200°C/Gas Mark 6, until they are collapsing, and then slightly burn the skins over a gas hob flame to create the smoky flavour.) Leave to cool.

When the aubergines are cool enough to handle, peel away and discard the skins. You will be left with a messy, smoky mass.

Put the aubergine flesh into the bowl of your food processor with the garlic, tahini and cumin and blend together. As the motor spins, pour in a slow, fine, steady stream of olive oil through the feeder tube to loosen the mix, give it a glossy shine and, of course, add flavour. About 1 tablespoon should do. Slowly incorporate half the lemon juice, a small pinch of sugar and a fair pinch of salt. Taste the mixture and add more lemon juice, sugar and salt as required. Set aside.

To make the flatbreads, combine everything in a bowl and bring the mixture together into a dough. Knead the dough for a couple of minutes. Allow it to rest for 5 minutes.

Divide the dough into 8 equal balls. Dust a board and rolling pin with a little flour. Squash the balls into fat discs in your palms, then roll them out into thin circles.

Cook 1 at a time, either in a very hot, dry frying pan over high heat, or over the hottest embers of a BBQ. Cook for about 30 seconds on each side – they should puff up and blister. Serve warm or cool with the babaganoush.

VIETNAMESE RICE PAPER ROLLS

SERVES 2

For the rolls
50g vermicelli rice noodles
8 good-sized leaves from a little
    gem lettuce (double up the
    leaves if some are too small)
1 carrot, sliced into thin strips
    with a vegetable peeler
½ cucumber, sliced into thin
    strips with a vegetable peeler
2 spring onions, thinly sliced
small bunch of mint
small bunch of coriander
small bunch of basil
60g mixed bean sprouts
    and seed sprouts
30g salted peanuts, chopped
8 rice paper wrappers

For the dipping sauce
1 teaspoon grated ginger
2 red bird's eye chillies,
    finely sliced
1 garlic clove, crushed
1 teaspoon light brown sugar
3 tablespoons soy sauce
    or tamari
lime juice, to taste

You might find the first few wraps a bit of a fiddle, as the rice paper is delicate. Be brave but gentle and you'll soon get into a rhythm. The filling is fresh, crisp and fragrant. All the seasoning and kick comes from the dipping sauce. There are plenty of protein-rich bean and seed sprouts available beyond your basic bean and alfalfa. Try radish, lentil, chickpea or broccoli sprouts, which can be bought in colourful mixed packs, too.

Place the noodles in a heatproof bowl and cover them with boiling water. Steep according to packet instructions, until just cooked through. Drain and cool immediately under running cold water. Keep to one side.

Fill the lettuce leaves with a mix of noodles, veg, herbs and sprouts. Finish with a sprinkle of peanuts. Set aside.

Fill a bowl with boiling water. Soak 1 rice paper wrapper in the water for about 10 seconds, until it becomes pliant. Lay it on a clean tea towel (they tend to stick to work surfaces) and sit a packed leaf horizontally on top. Fold in the bottom and sides of the wrapper, then roll it up like a cigar. Repeat with the remaining wrappers and packed leaves.

In a separate bowl, mix all the dipping sauce ingredients together, adding lime juice to your taste.

Serve the rolls whole or cut in half at an angle to reveal your meticulous and artistic packing, with the dipping sauce on the side. Dip and dine.

PEA & POTATO DOSA WITH RAITA

SERVES 2

For the dosa
50g rice flour
50g chickpea flour
170ml water
salt
sunflower or vegetable oil,
    for frying

For the filling
1 tablespoon oil
3 spring onions, sliced
500g boiled potatoes, diced
2 tomatoes, roughly chopped
1 garlic clove, chopped
1 green chilli, chopped
100g peas, defrosted
½ teaspoon turmeric
½ tablespoon garam masala
¼ teaspoon brown mustard seeds
½ teaspoon black onion seeds
lemon juice, to taste
small bunch of coriander,
    chopped
salt and pepper

For the raita
½ cucumber
200g vegan yogurt
small bunch of mint, chopped
pinch of salt

To serve (optional)
lime pickle
mango chutney

Who doesn't love a masala dosa? This recipe is a bit of a hack, as the batter is normally made with fermented rice, taking three days to process. But here you get insta-dosas. Try to make them as thin and crêpe-like as you can. It may be worth making a bit more batter than you need, so you can have a few practice runs. Also, the dosa can be made ahead of time and chilled or frozen. Stack them between sheets of baking paper and sit them on a plate, then wrap them up in a huge food bag to freeze. To serve, defrost them, then flip-flop them in a hot pan for 30 seconds until hot. Serve your dosa with this spicy pea and potato masala. This is comfort food, South Indian style.

Put the rice and chickpea flours into a mixing bowl with the water and whisk until you have a thin batter. Mix in a good pinch of salt. Transfer the mixture to the fridge and leave to rest for 30 minutes.

Meanwhile, prepare the pea and potato masala filling. Heat the oil in a frying pan and cook the spring onion gently over medium-low heat for 3–4 minutes, until starting to soften.

Add the potato, tomato, garlic and chilli to the frying pan. Season with salt and pepper. Cook for 10 minutes, until the potato begins to break up and the tomato cooks down.

Meanwhile, make the raita. Remove the soft, seedy core from the cucumber half with the tip of a teaspoon. Coarsely grate the flesh and give it a gentle squeeze over the sink to remove excess water. Mix it with the yogurt and mint in a bowl. Season with a pinch of salt.

When the cooking time for the potato mix has elapsed, mix in the peas, turmeric, garam masala and the mustard and onion seeds. Fry for 2–3 minutes, until everything smells fragrant. Taste and tweak the seasoning with salt, pepper and a squeeze or 2 of lemon. Stir in the coriander. Take the pan off the heat, cover and keep to one side while you make the dosas.

Remove the batter from the fridge and give it a whisk to refresh. Rub a small, shallow frying pan or crêpe pan with oil. Tip in a small ladleful of batter and swirl it round the pan to spread it out in a thin layer. Fry for 1 minute or so, until golden brown. Flip it gently and cook the other side for a further minute, until golden brown. Keep it warm and repeat until you have 4 good dosas.

Divide the filing between the 4 dosas and roll them up. Serve with the raita and some lime pickle and mango chutney, if you have any.

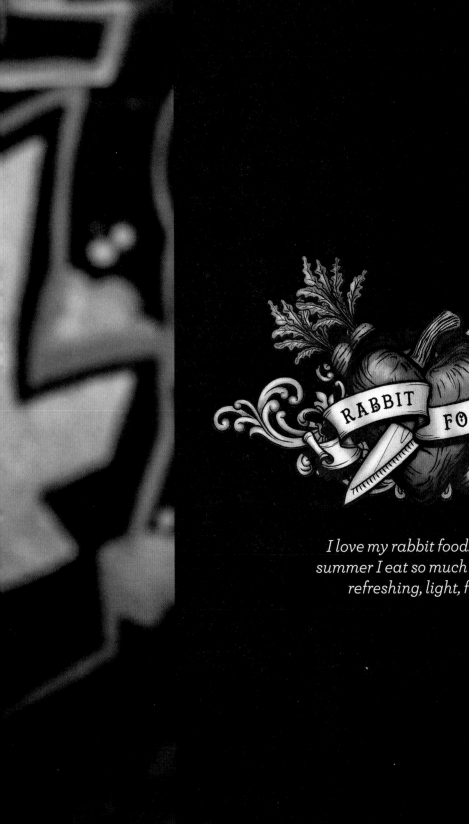

I love my rabbit food. In the summer I eat so much of this – refreshing, light, fast.

THE SCARLET SALAD
SERVES 4

For the marinade
2 oranges, segmented
    and juice collected
2 fennel bulbs, cut into
    wafer-thin slices
1 teaspoon paprika

For the dressing
4 tablespoons extra virgin
    olive oil
2 tablespoons white wine vinegar
1 teaspoon wholegrain mustard
1 small garlic clove, crushed
1 teaspoon maple syrup
salt and pepper

For the salad
3 tablespoons sunflower seeds
3 tablespoons pine nuts
150g Russian or regular kale
100g mixed salad leaves
½ a cucumber
300g rocket
10 cherry tomatoes, halved
handful of edible flowers

This went down a treat with the Scarlets Rugby Team as it's packed with flavour and colour, and the vinegary, garlicky dressing brings the leaves to life. I get my salad leaves from Cae Tan, a Community Supported Agricultural Project in South Wales. Using fresh, biodynamic produce makes an unbelievable difference to how much I enjoy a salad bowl.

Start with the marinade. Put the orange segments and juice into a bowl with the fennel slices as soon as you slice them (to stop them browning), then add the paprika and stir. Leave to stand, overnight ideally, or for as long as possible.

Put the sunflower seeds and pine nuts into a heavy-based pan and toast them over low heat for 5 minutes, until they take on a rich brown colour – be careful not to char them.

To make the dressing, put the ingredients into a bowl, season to taste and mix thoroughly. The mustard should emulsify the mixture to make a smooth dressing.

Next, prepare the Russian kale. This leaf is good raw, but the stems can be tough. Remove the stems and slice the leaves into bite-sized sections.

Put the salad leaves, the cucumber, kale, rocket and tomatoes into a serving bowl. Pour a half the dressing into the bowl and toss the salad by hand. Drain the fennel from the marinade, reserving a few orange slices for decoration, and add it to the bowl. Sprinkle over the sunflower seeds and pine nuts, arrange the orange slices on top, then drizzle the remaining dressing over the salad. Garnish with the edible flowers and serve immediately.

RAW SALAD

SERVES 2

1 red onion
5 radishes
¼ red cabbage
½ cucumber
5 tomatoes, chopped
1 avocado, chopped
2 carrots, grated
lemon juice, to taste
1 bag of rocket
½ iceberg lettuce, chopped
handful of cashews
handful of raisins

To garnish
1 tablespoon chia seeds,
   for sprinkling
1 tablespoon sesame seeds,
   for sprinkling

For the dressing
6 tablespoons olive oil
1 tablespoon sesame oil
1 teaspoon wholegrain mustard
2 tablespoons balsamic vinegar
1 teaspoon agave nectar
salt and pepper

Fresh, clean and delicious! This salad is packed with raw veg and paired with an amazing, zingy dressing. A fully raw dish requires a bit of chewing, which forces you to slow down and eat properly. And it's full of vitamins and minerals, as nothing has been lost through cooking. The mixture of all these flavours is like a party in your mouth! This is how veg should be eaten.

To make the dressing, grab an old jam jar, put all the dressing ingredients into it, put on the lid and shake (preferably to music). You should have a lovely dressing for your raw salad. Set aside.

A food processor with a slicing blade attachment is the perfect tool for making this salad – use a blade that will give you nice thin slices. If you don't have a food processor then I hope you're good with a knife. Grab the red onion, radish, red cabbage and cucumber and slice away, leaving you with a mound of loveliness.

Put your sliced veggies into a nice bowl, then add the chopped tomato and avocado and your grated carrot. Squeeze over some fresh lemon juice. Add the rocket, iceberg, cashews and raisins and mix together. Tip in the dressing and toss with your hands to coat all those lovely raw veggies and salad. Serve immediately.

AUBERGINE & TAHINI GIANT COUSCOUS SALAD

SERVES 2

200g cherry tomatoes, quartered
1 shallot, very finely sliced
1 teaspoon ground cumin
½ teaspoon ground cinnamon
2 pinches of salt, plus extra
    for salting
100g giant couscous
300ml boiling water
pinch of saffron threads or
    turmeric
2 aubergines, cut (widthways
    or lengthways) into 1-cm
    thick slices
olive oil, for frying
80g rocket or watercress
small bunch of mint, chopped
small bunch of flat-leaf parsley,
    chopped
30g flaked almonds, toasted
sumac, to garnish

For the tahini dressing
2 tablespoons tahini
1 small garlic clove,
    finely chopped
2 tablespoons lemon juice
½ teaspoon sugar
approximately 4 tablespoons
    hot water
salt

This satisfying salad combines some lovely flavours of the Middle East. Saffron may seem an expensive ingredient, but a little pinch goes a long way. As an alternative, use a pinch of turmeric for the colour. Giant couscous can come under many names and varieties – maftoul, ptitim, moghrabieh or Jerusalem couscous to name a few. Most of the supermarkets have settled on giant couscous to save headaches. It makes a fun alternative to the tiny couscous we all know and love.

Put a kettle on to boil.

Put the tomatoes into a mixing bowl with the shallot, cumin, cinnamon and a pinch of salt and mix together. Set aside to macerate while you get everything else ready.

Place the couscous in a saucepan with the saffron and a pinch of salt. Tip in the measured boiling water and stir. Simmer over a very gentle heat, stirring from time to time, for about 10 minutes or until cooked – check the packet, as cooking times may vary. The liquid should all be absorbed – add a dash more hot water if it looks as though the couscous is drying out. Spread out the cooked couscous on a plate and allow to cool.

While the couscous cooks, start cooking the aubergines. Lightly salt each side of each slice. Heat some olive oil in a large frying pan, add the aubergine slices and cook for

Recipe continued overleaf

Recipe continued

5–10 minutes, until golden on both sides and cooked through – you may need to do this in batches. You're going to use more oil than you think as the aubergine soaks it up like a sponge as it cooks. You'll want an all-purpose olive oil for this job. Don't go wasting the boutique stuff! (Alternatively, cook the seasoned slices on an un-oiled griddle pan until nicely char marked. Mix with olive oil and finish in a medium oven for 10 minutes to cook through.) Set aside.

To make the dressing, mix the tahini, garlic, lemon juice and sugar in a bowl. As you whisk, gradually add the measured hot water, adding more if needed, until the mixture reaches a yogurt-like consistency. It will look as though it is thickening and splitting at the start. Stay with it – it will come together in the end. Season well with salt.

Mix the couscous and salad leaves into the bowl with the tomatoes. Transfer the mixture to a large serving plate and tuck in the aubergine slices here and there. Artistically streak the dressing over the top and garnish with the herbs, almonds and a dusting of sumac. Serve straight away.

BRAISED RADISH, ASPARAGUS and BULGUR SALAD

SERVES 4

80g bulgur wheat
2 pinches of salt, plus
    extra to taste
1 tablespoon olive oil,
    plus extra to dress
200g radishes, trimmed
    and halved
2 tablespoons cider vinegar
200g asparagus, trimmed
2 courgettes
100g defrosted peas
2 spring onions, finely sliced
80g interesting mixed
    salad leaves
small bunch of mint, chopped
salt

For the dressing
1 small garlic clove, finely
    chopped
½ tablespoon Dijon mustard
1½ tablespoons lemon juice,
    or to taste
2 tablespoons olive oil
2 tablespoons sunflower oil
salt and pepper

Cook a radish? Give it a go! It mellows the raw peppery heat. And while you're at the stove you can griddle the asparagus, too. These flavours add depth to this fresh-tasting salad. But if all this braising and griddling seems like a faff, you can simply steam or boil the asparagus, and use raw sliced radishes instead.

Set a cast iron griddle pan on the hob over high heat to heat up. It will need at least 10 minutes to get to temperature. Boil a kettle.

Tip the bulgur wheat into a heatproof bowl or jug and add a pinch of salt. Pour over enough boiling water to cover the bulgur wheat by 2cm. Cover the bowl tightly with clingfilm and let stand for at least 20 minutes to allow the bulgur to cook and plump up. Set aside until needed.

Meanwhile, heat the oil in a saucepan. Add the radish with a pinch of salt and fry over medium heat for 2 minutes. Add the cider vinegar and clamp the lid on tight. Cook for a further 3–4 minutes, until there is still enough bite in the radish halves to keep them interesting – you don't want them mushy. They bleed their colour as they cook, turning the white parts bright pink. Remove the lid and let any excess liquid cook away for a minute or 2. Put to one side to cool.

Recipe continued overleaf

Recipe continued

Griddle the asparagus for 3 minutes or so, rolling occasionally to get char marks on all sides. Remove from the pan and oil and salt the spears lightly. Set aside to cool.

Use a vegetable peeler to slice the courgettes into long ribbon-like strips, stopping when you get to the seedy cores. Put the strips into a large bowl and discard the cores.

To make the dressing, whisk the garlic, mustard and lemon juice together in a small bowl or jug until smooth. Whisk in the oils a little at a time until you have a thick, emulsified dressing. Season to taste with salt, pepper and a little more lemon juice if needed.

Add the bulgur wheat, radish, asparagus, peas, spring onion, salad leaves and mint to the bowl with the courgettes and gently mix together. Arrange everything artfully on a serving plate and spoon over some of the dressing. Serve straight away.

SMASHED CUCUMBER and SOBA NOODLE SALAD

SERVES 4

250g green beans, trimmed
    and larger ones sliced in half
    at an angle
150g soba noodles
1 large or 3 mini cucumbers
3 spring onions, finely sliced
60g pea shoots
small bunch of coriander,
    chopped
few sprigs of mint, chopped
lime juice, to taste

For the dressing
4 tablespoons sesame oil
2 tablespoons sweet white miso
2 tablespoons rice wine vinegar
½ tablespoon tamari or soy sauce

To garnish
40g salted peanuts,
    roughly chopped
½ tablespoon toasted sesame
    seeds
1 red chilli, deseeded and
    finely chopped

Channel your aggressions into making this yummy salad. Smashing the cucumber creates more nooks, crannies and craggy surface area for the delicious dressing to cling to. The dressing's salt draws out liquid from the cucumbers, which thins it down nicely and adds to the flavour.

Cook the beans in a pan of salted, boiling water for about 3 minutes, or until just cooked. Remove with a slotted spoon and cool immediately in cold water. Drain well.

Cook the noodles in the same water according to the packet instructions until just done. Drain and cool immediately under running cold water. Drain and keep to one side.

For the dressing, use a fork to mix all the ingredients together in a mixing bowl.

Place the cucumber in a plastic bag and tap it, somewhat aggressively, with a rolling pin until its surfaces are a little crushed. Empty out the contents of the bag onto a chopping board and cut it into rough chunks. Place these in the mixing bowl with the dressing, mix well and leave to macerate for 10 minutes at least.

To finish, add the beans, noodles, spring onions, pea shoots and herbs to the bowl. Mix well, taste and tweak the flavour with a squeeze or 2 of lime juice to your liking.

Pile the salad onto a serving plate and garnish with peanuts, sesame seeds and chopped chilli. Serve immediately.

CAULIFLOWER, APPLE and RADICCHIO SALAD

SERVES 2

1 cauliflower, cut into
1-cm thick slices
olive oil
lemon juice, to taste
100g quinoa
300ml boiling water
2 pinches of salt, plus
extra to taste
1 small head of radicchio
lettuce (or use chicory
or endive), torn
2 tablespoons red wine vinegar
1 large apple, cored and diced
2 celery sticks, finely sliced
40g toasted walnuts,
roughly chopped

For the caper dressing
½ tablespoon Dijon mustard
large handful of chopped parsley
2 tablespoons capers, finely
chopped
olive oil, to taste

There's a lot going on in this salad. It's a tangy, crunchy riot of flavours and textures in a bowl. The sweetness from the apple should balance out the bitter notes of the radicchio.

Preheat the oven to 200°C (Gas Mark 6). Put a kettle on to boil.

Place the cauliflower slices in a roasting tray. Coat them in oil, then season well with salt and pepper and add a good squeeze of lemon juice. Roast for 15 minutes, until nicely coloured and tender. Leave to cool a little.

Meanwhile, warm the quinoa in a dry saucepan over medium heat for 3–4 minutes, until toasting and starting to pop. Add the measured boiling water and a pinch of salt. Cook for 12 minutes, until the water has been absorbed and the grains are cooked. Tip into a sieve and cool under running cold water. Leave to drain.

Throw the radicchio into a mixing bowl with the vinegar and a pinch of salt. Toss together and leave to rest.

To make the caper dressing, mix the mustard, parsley and capers together in a jug with enough olive oil to give you a loose pesto consistency.

Add the quinoa and cauliflower to the bowl of radicchio, then add the apple and celery and mix well. Pile the salad onto a serving plate. To finish, scatter over the toasted walnuts and spoon over the caper dressing.

SWEETCORN, SQUASH and BLACK RICE SALAD

SERVES 2–3

1 small butternut squash,
    peeled and cut into
    2-cm chunks
olive oil
1 large red pepper
2 sweetcorn cobs, husks
    removed
150g black rice or wild rice
small bunch of coriander,
    chopped
2 spring onions, finely sliced
salt and pepper

For the Mexican dressing
1 small garlic clove, crushed
1 teaspoon ground cumin
½ teaspoon ground coriander
½ teaspoon dried oregano
½ teaspoon light brown sugar
juice of 1 lime
3 tablespoons olive oil
chipotle chilli flakes, to taste

Substantial and satisfying, this is perfect for those cold evenings when your body wants some serious carb. Cook the corn (in its husks), peppers and squash on a BBQ for a deeper, smokier flavour. You can add half a can of cooked black or kidney beans to the final mix for a boost of protein.

Preheat the oven to 200°C (Gas Mark 6).

Place the squash chunks in a roasting tray and season and oil generously. Rub the pepper with oil and add to the tray. Roast for 25–30 minutes, until the squash is cooked and the pepper blisters. Remove from the oven and leave to cool.

Meanwhile, lower the cobs into a pan of boiling salted water and boil for 8–10 minutes, until tender. Remove and leave to cool.

Tip the rice into the boiling water. Simmer for 35–40 minutes, until tender (wild rice will retain a distinct bite to it). Drain and cool under running cold water.

Mix the dressing ingredients together in a big mixing bowl.

Hold a sweetcorn cob vertically and run a small serrated knife from top to bottom to cut the kernels away, repeating all the way around the cob and then with the other cob.

Break open the pepper and discard the seeds. Strip away and discard the skin and roughly chop the flesh.

Tip all the ingredients into the bowl of dressing. Mix well and serve.

PIRI PIRI TOMATO and CRISPY CHICKPEA SALAD

SERVES 2

350g mixed cherry and baby
  plum tomatoes, halved or
  quartered (depending on size)
olive oil
400g can chickpeas (reserve
  the liquid to use as aquafaba
  in other recipes)
1 small red onion, finely sliced
60g rocket or watercress
salt and pepper
small bunch of flat-leaf or curly
  parsley, chopped, to garnish

For the dressing
1 red chilli, finely chopped
1 small garlic clove, finely
  chopped
1 teaspoon freshly chopped
  oregano or thyme leaves
2 tablespoons red wine vinegar
1 tablespoon vegan
  Worcestershire sauce
1 teaspoon smoked paprika
2 tablespoons olive oil
1½ tablespoons lemon juice
cayenne pepper, to taste
  (optional)
salt and pepper

Roasting chickpeas transforms them into incredibly moreish, crisp, nutty nuggets, while roasting tomatoes intensifies their sweet flavour. A cracking pairing!

Preheat the oven to 150°C (Gas Mark 2).

Lay the tomatoes, with their cut sides facing up, on a baking tray. Drizzle with oil and season with salt. Transfer to the oven and cook slowly for 1 hour, until starting to colour at the edges. Remove and set aside to cool.

Increase the oven temperature to 200°C (Gas Mark 6). Drain the chickpeas. Tip them onto a clean tea towel and pat them dry as much as you can. Place them in a roasting tray, then oil and season them well. Spread them out so they sit in a single layer. Roast for 20 minutes, turning twice during cooking, until deep golden – remove them from the oven early if they look like they are burning.

To make the dressing, mix the ingredients in a large bowl, seasoning to taste. Add some cayenne pepper if the dressing needs more oomph!

Put the chickpeas, onion and rocket or watercress into the bowl with the dressing and mix. Pile the salad onto a serving dish and scatter over the roasted tomatoes and a sprinkle of parsley. Serve immediately, before the chickpeas go soggy.

BELLY WARMERS

*I spend most of my winter feasting on these.
Soup is so easy, and so good for you when
you get the ingredients right. This section is
the height of comfort food. Fill your boots.*

RIBOLLITA WITH CHOPPING BOARD PESTO

SERVES 2–3

For the croûtons

3 thick slices of sourdough
  bread or ciabatta, crusts
  discarded and bread torn
  into bite-sized chunks
olive oil
salt

For the ribollita

2 tablespoons olive oil
1 onion, finely diced
1 celery stick, finely diced
1 carrot, finely diced
1 garlic clove, crushed
1 teaspoon finely
  chopped rosemary
1 bay leaf
1 tablespoon tomato purée
400g can chopped tomatoes
1 tablespoon balsamic vinegar
400g can cannellini, borlotti
  or haricot beans
700ml vegetable stock
200g kale, woody stems
  removed and leaves
  roughly chopped
salt and pepper

For the pesto

40g basil leaves
30g toasted pine nuts
1 garlic clove
zest of ½ lemon
3 tablespoons olive oil

This thrifty Italian soup combines leftovers into a new meal. Traditionally, stale bread was added as a bulker, but can get a bit mushy – I'd rather have the texture of a crispy croûton. My speedy pesto does away with the pestle and mortar. Think of it less as a paste, more as a pesto-esque garnish.

To make the croûtons, preheat the oven to 200°C (Gas Mark 6). Toss the bread with oil and salt on a shallow baking tray. Bake for 10–12 minutes, turning halfway, until golden and crisp. (These can be stored in an airtight container.)

For the ribollita, heat the olive oil in a large saucepan. Add the onion, celery and carrots and cook gently over medium-low heat for 10 minutes, until starting to soften.

Add the garlic, rosemary and bay leaf to the saucepan. Cook for 2 minutes more, then stir in the tomato purée, chopped tomatoes, vinegar, beans and stock. Season with salt and pepper and bring to a gentle simmer for 10 minutes. Stir the kale into the stew and cook gently for a further 20 minutes.

While the soup cooks, place the basil leaves on a chopping board with the pine nuts, garlic and lemon zest. Chop everything together until you have a crumbly green pile. Place it in a bowl and stir in the oil.

When the soup is cooked, taste and tweak the seasoning to your liking. Serve with a tumble of croûtons and plenty of pesto on top.

INDIAN CAULIFLOWER, SPINACH and LENTIL SOUP

SERVES 2

2 tablespoons sunflower
  or vegetable oil
1 onion, sliced
1 celery stick, diced
pinch of salt, plus extra to taste
1 potato, diced
2 tomatoes, roughly chopped
1 garlic clove, crushed
½ tablespoon freshly grated
  ginger
1 tablespoon medium curry
  powder
½ teaspoon yellow mustard seeds
½ teaspoon fennel seeds
½ teaspoon nigella seeds
½ tablespoon curry leaves
50g red lentils, rinsed
600ml vegetable stock
1 cauliflower, broken
  into small florets
30g desiccated coconut
100g spinach
lemon juice, to taste
pepper

*Don't let the long list of ingredients put you off this soup –
it doesn't take that long as you are just chucking all the
spices in at once. It's full of cracking flavour and well
worth the effort.*

Heat the oil in a saucepan over medium-low heat. Gently fry
the onion and celery with a pinch of salt for 5 minutes, until
starting to soften. Add the potato, tomato, garlic, ginger and
spices and fry for 5 minutes more, stirring well to stop the
spices sticking (add a splash of water if necessary).

Stir the lentils into the saucepan and add the stock. Bring
the mixture to a simmer and cook for 10 minutes.

Now mix the cauliflower florets into the saucepan and
cook for a further 20 minutes, until both the cauliflower
and lentils are soft. Stir in a little water if the mixture
looks as though it is becoming too thick.

While the soup cooks, heat the coconut in a frying pan
over low heat for about 5 minutes until lightly toasted.
Set aside.

When the cooking time for the soup has elapsed, stir in
the spinach and cook for a couple of minutes more, until the
leaves are completely wilted. Taste the soup and tweak the
seasoning with salt, pepper and some generous squeezes
of lemon juice. Serve dusted with the toasted coconut.

WATERCRESS, BROCCOLI and SPINACH SOUP

SERVES 4

olive oil
1 onion, finely chopped
2 garlic cloves, finely chopped
1.5 litres vegetable stock
2 potatoes, diced
1 head of broccoli, chopped
300g watercress
1 bag of spinach
salt and pepper

To garnish
oat cream
flat-leaf or curly parsley,
   finely chopped

Green, green and more greenery! I love all things green, and this tasty green soup is a bowlful of good health. Another bonus is that it's so easy to make. Great to share with the family, and I like to put any leftovers into a flask to take out with me when I'm on the go.

Heat a little oil in a deep saucepan. Add the onion and garlic and fry over medium-low heat for 5 minutes, until beginning to soften.

Add the stock, potato and broccoli to the saucepan and cook for about 15 minutes, until tender.

Stir in the watercress and spinach and cook for only 2–3 minutes (so they retain lots of nutrients), until wilted. Take the pan off the heat, grab a hand blender and blend the soup in the pan (or tip the soup into a blender, blitz, then pour it back into the saucepan). Whisk the soup, season and serve, garnished with oat cream and a sprinkling of parsley.

ROAST SQUASH and RED PEPPER SOUP

SERVES 4

½ any squash (about 500g, halved lengthways), deseeded
3 red peppers, halved and deseeded
4 carrots, halved lengthways
4 red onions, halved
olive oil
2 garlic bulbs
up to 1.2 litres vegetable stock
2 tablespoons coconut milk
salt and pepper
bread, to serve

This soup will keep your belly warm and give you a nice cosy feeling. Eating it in winter is like being curled up with your dog in a duvet next to a fire! Roasting the veg first intensifies their flavours – you can really taste the difference. It takes a bit more time, but it doesn't really require any more effort than making a soup without the roasting step.

Preheat the oven to 200°C (Gas Mark 6).

Place your squash in a roasting tin with the cut side facing upwards. Add the peppers, carrots and red onion. Lightly oil and season with salt and pepper. Slice a few millimetres off the top of the garlic bulbs so you can just see a little of the flesh of the garlic cloves inside their papery skins. Tuck the trimmed bulbs into the tray. Roast for 35–40 minutes, until the squash flesh is cooked through.

Once removed from the oven and cool enough to touch, squeeze each garlic clove individually to push the roasted flesh from the skin. Use a spoon to scoop out the squash flesh and put it into a blender or the bowl of a food processor with the remaining roasted veg, garlic flesh and half the stock. Blitz then blend in as much of the remaining stock as you need to give your soup the texture you prefer.

Transfer the soup to a saucepan, passing it through a sieve first if you don't like bits in your soup. Adjust the seasoning and stir in the coconut milk to give it a creamy texture. Heat gently, then serve with some lovely bread.

MEXICAN SOUP, AVOCADO SALSA and TORTILLA CHIPS

SERVES 4

For the soup
olive oil, for frying
1 onion, diced
1 red pepper, sliced
1 garlic clove, crushed
½ tablespoon ground cumin
½ tablespoon ground coriander
½ teaspoon ground cinnamon
½ teaspoon dried chipotle
    chilli flakes
500ml vegetable stock
150g passata
400g can kidney beans
½ tablespoon light brown sugar
pinch of salt, plus extra to taste
pinch of pepper, plus extra
    to taste

For the tortilla chips
4 corn tortillas
sunflower or vegetable oil,
    for brushing
salt

For the salsa
1 avocado, diced
1 spring onion, finely chopped
handful of chopped coriander
1 red chilli, finely chopped
lime juice, to taste
salt, to taste

This hearty soup is full of sunny flavours and a hit of spice. Making your own tortilla chips is dead easy and adds a bit of fun to the whole thing.

Preheat the oven to 180°C (Gas Mark 4).

Heat some oil in a saucepan, add the onion and pepper and fry over medium heat for 10 minutes, until they begin to soften. Stir in the garlic, cumin, coriander, cinnamon and chilli and fry for a further 2 minutes, stirring continuously so that the spices don't stick and burn.

Tip the stock and passata into the pan along with the kidney beans and their liquid. Add the sugar and a good pinch of salt and pepper. Bring the mixture to a simmer and cook gently over medium-low heat for 20 minutes.

Meanwhile, make the tortilla chips. Brush each tortilla with oil on both sides . Cut each into 12 wedges and sprinkle with a little salt. Lay out the wedges evenly on a baking tray. Bake for 4 minutes, then turn over and cook for a further 4 minutes or until they are just starting to colour and become crisp. Remove from the oven and set aside.

To make the salsa, mix the ingredients together in a bowl.

When the soup is cooked, blend or process it until smooth. Check and tweak the seasoning as desired. Serve topped with the salsa, with the tortilla chips on the side.

OKRA and GREEN BEAN GUMBO

SERVES 4

olive oil
2 red onions, diced
2 celery sticks, diced
2 green peppers, diced
150g okra, sliced
100g green beans, finely sliced
1 small sweet potato, peeled
    and diced
½ tablespoon thyme leaves
½ tablespoon smoked paprika
3 garlic cloves, chopped
1 bay leaf
400g tomatoes, roughly chopped
    (or 400g can chopped
    tomatoes)
2 tablespoons vegan
    Worcestershire sauce
800ml vegetable stock
cayenne pepper, to taste
salt and pepper

To garnish
1 spring onion, finely sliced
small handful of chopped parsley
1 red chilli, finely chopped
1 lime, cut into wedges
fried slices of Chorizo Seitan
    Sausage (see page 145)
    (optional)

Gumbo is a stew that originates from America's Southern states. It always contains a base of what is referred to over there as the holy trinity of veggies – onions, bell peppers and celery. Good start! Okra is prized for its curious thickening quality in a stew. It can be an acquired taste and may be hard to find. Asian groceries are a good bet. If you can't get hold of any, substitute a diced courgette, and cook 2 tablespoons plain flour into the veg before adding any liquid. You can turn this into a full-on main meal by serving it with rice, quinoa or polenta.

Heat the oil in a large saucepan. Throw in the onion, celery, pepper and okra. Cook gently over medium-low heat for 10 minutes, until starting to soften.

Add the green beans, sweet potato, thyme, paprika, garlic and bay leaf to the saucepan and mix well. Cook for 2 minutes more, then stir in the tomatoes, Worcestershire sauce and stock. Bring to a simmer. Season with salt, pepper and as much cayenne pepper as you fancy – you can always add more at the end. Simmer for 25 minutes, or until everything is tender, stirring in a little water if at any time it looks as though the stew is drying out.

When ready, taste and tweak the seasoning. Serve with some spring onions, parsley and fresh chilli, if you'd like more heat. Give each person a lime wedge for squeezing. Some slices of chorizo seitan, fried until crisp, make a great addition too.

ROASTED TOMATO SOUP

SERVES 4

450g tomatoes, halved
olive oil
1 garlic bulb
3 red onions, quartered
2 celery sticks, roughly chopped
1 teaspoon vegan
   Worcester sauce
2 tablespoons balsamic vinegar
1 litre vegetable stock
1 potato, diced
salt and pepper
basil leaves, to serve
soya cream, to serve

There's nothing like this – it's what my Mam gave us when we were ill! I love watching the tomatoes roast away in the oven, building up their flavour for this delicious dish. It's great cold in the summer, too.

Preheat the oven to 180°C (Gas Mark 4).

Put the halved tomatoes and onion quarters into a baking tray and cover with oil. Slice a few millimetres off the top of the garlic bulb so you can just see a little flesh of the garlic cloves inside their papery skins. Sit the bulb next to the tomatoes in the tray. Roast for 30 minutes, until everything is nicely roasted.

Meanwhile, heat a little oil in a saucepan. Add the celery and fry over medium-low heat for 5–7 minutes, until lightly golden. Set aside until the tomato and garlic are ready.

When the tomatoes and onions are done, add them to the celery in the saucepan with the vegan Worcester sauce and balsamic vinegar. Wrap a clean tea towel around your fingers, pick up the roasted garlic bulb and squeeze each garlic clove individually to push out the roasted garlic flesh from the skin and into the pan. Mix it all together.

Pour the stock into the pan, mix in the potato, then simmer for 15 minutes, until the potatoes are cooked. Take the pan off the heat and blend the soup with a hand blender, then season to your liking. Serve with basil leaves on top and as much soya cream as you'd like to taste. Personally, I just sprinkle a little over the top of my soup.

MISO BROTH

SERVES 2

sunflower or vegetable oil
10 spring onions, chopped
   at an angle
1 red chilli, finely chopped
2.5cm piece of fresh root ginger,
   finely chopped
2 garlic cloves, finely chopped
125g shiitake mushrooms,
   cut into bite-sized pieces
1 litre vegetable stock
400g firm tofu, diced
1 teaspoon miso paste
2 nori sheets (optional),
   folded and sliced into shreds,
   plus extra to garnish
300g udon noodles
2 radishes, finely sliced,
   to garnish
pepper

*Comforting and deeply savoury, a miso broth always goes
down well, and a bowlful of noodles provides a good carb
hit to give you a kick up the arse when you need one. There's
just a bit of veg prep involved, but then you just throw it
all together and let the mixture simmer away into a tasty
noodle soup. Miso-hungry...*

Heat a little oil in a wok. Add the spring onion, chilli,
ginger and garlic and fry over medium heat for 5 minutes,
until softened. Mix in the mushrooms and cook for another
3 minutes. Add the veg stock and tofu dice, then stir in the
miso paste and the nori, if using. Mix well.

Add the noodles to the wok and simmer for 1–2 minutes,
until the noodles are cooked through. Serve immediately,
garnished with the sliced radish.

*These recipes are for when you are having
a bit more of a sit down after a hard day working,
training or whatever. This is your main treat of the day
which, in my case, calls for cracking open a bottle
of wine. If, like me, you tend to get carried away,
you might end up cracking open another.*

COURGETTE SPAGHETTI and AVOCADO PESTO

SERVES 2

3 courgettes, spiralized
150g cherry tomatoes, halved
¼ cucumber, diced
red chilli flakes, to taste
salt and pepper

For the pesto
1 avocado
good handful of basil leaves
½ tablespoon good-quality
   olive oil
1 garlic clove
1 tablespoon nutritional yeast
3 tablespoons lemon juice

This one is properly green and mean! It's really easy to make and is totally raw. This dish is full of good fats from the avocado, but it's potent on the garlic front, so be careful! There's no pasta – the spaghetti is made from spiralized strands of raw courgette. If you don't have a spiralizer, use a vegetable peeler to slice some nice, fine strips of courgette instead.

As soon as you have spiralized the courgettes, put them into a bowl and season with a generous amount of salt and pepper. Transfer to the fridge and leave for 30 minutes.

While the courgette does its thing in the fridge make the pesto. Combine the ingredients to a smooth paste using a food processor. Set aside.

After the salting time, rinse the courgettes and pat them dry. Put them into a large bowl, add the pesto and mix well. Now mix in the cherry tomatoes and cucumber and sprinkle with red chilli flakes to give the spaghetti a little heat kick. Dive in and enjoy.

CRISPY BANG BANG TOFU, PEANUT and CHILLI STIR-FRY

SERVES 2

120g udon noodles
3 tablespoons cornflour
pinch of salt
200g firm tofu, cut into 1-cm dice
2 tablespoons vegetable oil
2cm piece of fresh root ginger,
    finely grated
1 garlic clove, finely chopped
1 red chilli, deseeded and
    finely chopped
kernels from 1 small
    sweetcorn cob (or a handful
    of canned kernels)
1 carrot, cut into fine ribbons
    with a vegetable peeler
1 courgette, cut into fine ribbons
    with a vegetable peeler
100g mange tout or green beans,
    thinly sliced
small handful of coriander,
    chopped
½ lime, cut into wedges,
    to garnish

For the peanut sauce
2 tablespoons peanut butter
2 tablespoons soy sauce
    or tamari
1 tablespoon toasted sesame oil
juice of ½ lime

I love this speedy stir-fry. It's packed with colour and loads of beautiful veg. The cornflour gives the tofu a nice crispiness. You can do it without it, it'll just take longer to colour.

Cook the noodles in a saucepan of boiling water according to the packet instructions. Cool immediately in cold running water and drain well.

To make the sauce, whisk together the ingredients in a small bowl. Add a dash of hot water if it seems too thick. Set aside.

Put the cornflour and salt into a shallow bowl and mix together. Add the tofu dice and give them a couple of turns to coat them in the seasoned flour. Remove and shake away excess flour.

Heat the oil in a wok or large frying pan. Add the coated tofu dice and stir-fry over a high heat for 3–4 minutes, until the cubes are coloured well on all sides. Remove the cubes from the wok and set aside.

Return the wok to the heat, add the ginger, garlic, chilli and sweetcorn. Stir-fry for 1 minute then add the carrot, courgette and mange tout and stir-fry for another 2 minutes. Take the wok off the heat.

Add the tofu, noodles, peanut sauce and coriander to the wok and toss everything together to warm through. Serve with lime wedges for squeezing.

SWEET POTATO, DAHL and SPINACH GRATIN

SERVES 4

vegetable or sunflower oil,
    for frying
1 onion, sliced
1 teaspoon yellow mustard seeds
3 garlic cloves, sliced
250g red lentils, rinsed
2–3 dried chillies, crumbled
    (optional)
4 tomatoes, roughly chopped
800ml coconut milk
250g spinach
700g sweet potatoes,
    cut into 5-mm thick slices
salt and pepper

For the curry powder
½ tablespoon garam masala
1 teaspoon turmeric
1 teaspoon ground coriander
1 teaspoon ground ginger
½ teaspoon ground fenugreek

To serve
naan breads
Indian chutneys and pickles
Raita (optional, see page 62)

This is a hearty and complete meal in a tray – all your greens, protein, fats and carbs in one delicious dish. The gratin mixture seems very wet when it goes into the oven, but don't worry – it'll thicken as the lentils plump up and absorb the coconut milk. If chilli isn't your thing, omit it and leave the whole thing mild and fragrant. I've added a recipe for curry powder here, but if you want, simply use 1½ tablespoons of a good-quality, shop-bought mild curry powder instead.

Preheat the oven to 180°C (Gas Mark 4) and shake together the curry powder ingredients in a small jar.

Warm some oil in a saucepan. Add the onion and mustard seed and cook gently over medium-low heat for 10 minutes, until starting to soften. Stir in the garlic, lentils and chillies and cook for 2 minutes, then mix in the curry powder, tomatoes and coconut milk. Bring the mixture to a simmer, season well with salt and pepper and cook for 10 minutes.

Meanwhile, wilt the spinach in a dry frying pan for 1–2 minutes. Tip away any excess water and discard.

Spread the spinach across the base of a large gratin dish. Top with the lentil mixture then with the sweet potatoes in an overlapping shingle pattern. Bake for 30 minutes, until the potatoes are tender and coloured at the edges.

Serve immediately with naan breads and plenty of Indian chutneys, pickles and raita on the side.

JACKFRUIT and RED PEPPER GOULASH

SERVES 3~4

1 onion, sliced

2 red peppers, deseeded
   and sliced

4 tablespoons sunflower
   or vegetable oil

2 garlic cloves, finely chopped

2 tablespoons tomato purée

1 teaspoon caraway seeds

1 teaspoon dried oregano

400g can chopped tomatoes

400g can chickpeas (reserve
   the liquid to use as aquafaba
   in other recipes)

400ml vegetable stock

small pinch of cayenne pepper,
   plus extra to taste

400g can young jackfruit,
   cut into chunks

1 tablespoon plain flour

2 tablespoons sweet paprika
   (don't use smoked – it will
   dominate the flavour
   of the dish)

lemon juice, to taste

salt and pepper

To serve

small bunch of dill, chopped,
   to garnish

the carb of your choice

Jackfruit is becoming increasingly popular for vegans and vegetarians because its fibrous texture apes that of slow-cooked meat. Dusting it in seasoned flour and frying it deepens the flavour of the dish and adds to the texture. Serve this stew with mash, pasta, noodles or dumplings.

Gently cook the onion and peppers in half the oil, over medium-low heat, for 15 minutes, until softened. Add the garlic, tomato purée, caraway and oregano to the pan and cook for 2 minutes, then tip in in the tomato, drained chickpeas and stock. Season with salt and pepper and a small pinch of cayenne for warmth. Bring to a simmer and cook for 30 minutes. Add a dash more water if the mixture looks as though it is drying out or thickening too much.

Meanwhile, season the jackfruit chunks with salt and pepper. Mix the flour and paprika in a shallow bowl, coat the jackfruit chunks and shake away excess flour.

Heat the remaining oil in a frying pan. Add the coated jackfruit and fry over medium–high heat until nicely browned on all sides. Add to the goulash with any of the remaining flour and paprika mix. The goulash should still have 15–20 minutes left to cook, so let it simmer away while you relax for a while.

When the goulash is done, taste and add salt, pepper or cayenne, and add a squeeze or 2 of lemon to your taste. Garnish with the dill and serve with your carb of choice.

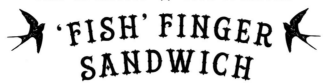

'FISH' FINGER SANDWICH

MAKES 4

4 crusty white rolls, to serve
2 beef tomatoes, sliced, to serve
    (optional)

For the sandwich slaw
4 tablespoons Vegan Mayo
    (see page 175)
1 tablespoon tomato ketchup
1 little gem lettuce,
    finely shredded
1 large carrot, coarsely grated
2 spring onions, finely sliced
2 tablespoons finely
    chopped capers
2 tablespoons finely
    chopped gherkins
small bunch of dill,
    finely chopped
small bunch of parsley,
    finely chopped
pinch of cayenne pepper
lemon juice, to taste
salt and pepper

For the 'fish' fingers
4 tablespoons cornflour
liquid from 400g can
    chickpeas (aquafaba)
15g dried seaweed flakes
30g panko breadcrumbs
400g very firm marinated
    tofu (see page 52), cut
    into 16 chunky batons
vegetable oil, for deep frying
generous pinch of salt

Seaweed gives these deep-fried tofu fingers a fishy quality. The Pembrokeshire Beach Food Company and the Cornish Seaweed Company both do good seaweed flakes but you can substitute finely chopped nori too.

To make the slaw, mix together the mayo and ketchup. Then add the remaining ingredients, season with salt, pepper and a squeeze or two of lemon juice and mix well.

To make the 'fish' fingers, tip the cornflour into a shallow bowl and the aquafaba into another. In a third bowl, mix the seaweed, breadcrumbs and a generous pinch of salt. Coat the tofu batons in the cornflour, shaking off any excess. Working 1 piece at a time, dip them into the aquafaba then the breadcrumbs. Press and turn until evenly coated.

Slowly bring 5cm of oil up to temperature for deep frying (around 190°C if you have a thermometer) in a high-sided saucepan. Carefully lower the tofu fingers in and fry for 3–4 minutes, until golden and crisp. You'll need to do this in batches of no more than 6 at a time or the oil temperature will drop too much. Remove carefully with a slotted spoon and transfer to a plate lined with kitchen paper to drain. Keep the cooked 'fish' fingers warm in a low oven while you fry the rest.

Spit the rolls open and pile in a generous amount of the slaw. Top with the 'fish' fingers and tomatoes, if using. Scoff while hot!

CHICKPEA CURRY

SERVES 2

rapeseed oil, for frying
1 teaspoon cumin seeds
5 garlic cloves, minced
1 thumb-sized piece fresh
    root ginger, minced
2 onions, chopped
2 bay leaves
700g passata
1 red or green chilli (use more
    and keep the seeds if you like
    your curry hotter), chopped
1 teaspoon turmeric
1 teaspoon ground coriander
1 teaspoon chilli powder
1 teaspoon ground cumin
1 teaspoon garam masala
400g can chickpeas
1 tablespoon lemon juice,
    or to taste
2 teaspoons sugar or 1 teaspoon
    agave nectar
small bunch of coriander
salt and pepper
cooked wild basmati rice,
    quinoa, buckwheat or
    potatoes, to serve

This is my numero uno curry recipe! The meaty texture of the chickpeas is very satisfying, while the subtle heat of the spices gives the dish that lovely Indian kiss. What's more, it's a store-cupboard meal that requires very little work, so is perfect for those weekday evenings when you're too tired to cook up a storm and your head is too scrambled to have even thought about dinner.

Heat a little oil in a saucepan, then add the cumin seeds, garlic, ginger and onion and fry over medium heat for about 4 minutes, until the onion is browned.

Add the bay leaves, then the passata to the saucepan. Now mix in all the spices. (If needed, add a little water to the mix to loosen it all up.) Next, add the chickpeas and stir well. Mix in the lemon juice and sugar or agave nectar and season with salt and pepper. Adjust the heat to get the mixture simmering gently and leave to simmer from about 30 minutes – the longer you leave it, the better it will taste! (Now's the time to cook your rice, potatoes or whatever you're serving the curry with.) Add the coriander roughly 5 minutes before dishing up, otherwise it wilts too much and you lose all the flavour.

PUTTANESCA AUBERGINE PARMIGIANA

SERVES 4–6

olive oil, for frying
2 red onions, sliced
2 garlic cloves, finely chopped
175ml white wine
1 tablespoon tomato purée
2 x 400g cans chopped tomatoes
2 tablespoons capers, chopped
100g green olives, sliced
200ml water
4 aubergines, cut lengthways
   into 1-cm thick slices
20g basil leaves, torn
50g sourdough breadcrumbs
1 tablespoon nutritional
   yeast flakes
zest of ½ a lemon
pinch of salt
80g vegan mozzarella,
   torn (optional)
pepper

This pepped-up parmigiana is an approximation of another Italian classic, puttanesca. Mind you don't over-season the sauce – the capers and olives bring plenty of salt to the show. Nutritional yeast adds a deep savoury flavour to the crumb.

Heat 2 tablespoons oil in a frying pan and cook the onion over medium-low heat for 10 minutes, until starting to soften. Stir in the garlic, wine and tomato purée, then let the mixture bubble away until reduced by half. Stir in the chopped tomatoes, capers, olives and measured water. Simmer for 20 minutes, until the sauce is thick and rich. Preheat the oven to 190°C (Gas Mark 5).

While the sauce cooks, heat some olive oil in a large frying pan and fry the aubergine, turning, over medium heat until golden and cooked through. (You'll use more oil than you think as the slices soak it up as they cook.) Set aside.

When the sauce is ready, mix in the basil leaves. Taste and tweak the seasoning as desired.

In a food processer, pulse together the breadcrumbs, yeast flakes, lemon zest, a pinch of salt and 1 tablespoon oil.

Lay half the aubergines into a large (about 30 x 20cm) baking dish and top with half the sauce. Repeat the layering process to fill the dish. Tear the mozzarella over the top, if using. Top evenly with the breadcrumb mix. Bake for 20–40 minutes, until the top is golden and the aubergine is tender.
Pictured overleaf

RAW AVOCADO and BASIL (OR DILL!) PASTA

SERVES 2

1 ripe avocado
few sprigs of basil (or use
    dill, but go easy with it
    – 4 fronds is enough)
2–3 garlic cloves
proper handful of rocket
approximately 500ml cashew
    cream or almond milk
salt and pepper
cooked spaghetti
    (or whichever pasta
    you like), to serve
chia seeds, to garnish

A raw sauce sounds mad, but this works. It tastes amazing and, even better, you are getting so much more of the nutrients from the veg by not cooking them - so celebrate the good stuff! We have a massive pasta party before every Ironman event and this dish always goes down well.

It's too easy. When you put your pasta on to cook, make your sauce. Put all the ingredients into the bowl of a food processor and whizz to a smooth consistency. Add a small amount of the pasta cooking water if the sauce is too thick and you're running low on almond milk or cashew cream. Taste the sauce and season to your liking, adding more garlic or herbs to suit you.

Combine with the cooked pasta, chuck on some chia seeds for a bit of added omega 3, and you're off.

ARTICHOKES and WHITE BEAN LINGUINE

SERVES 2

3 tablespoons olive oil,
   plus a glug extra
2 shallots, finely diced
1 celery stick, finely diced
pinch of salt, plus extra
   as desired
2 garlic cloves, finely chopped
175ml white wine
400g can cannellini beans
200ml vegetable stock
2 sprigs of thyme
1 bay leaf
200g cooked and marinated
   artichoke hearts, sliced
lemon juice, to taste (optional)
200g linguine or other
   long pasta
pepper
small bunch of parsley,
   chopped, to garnish

A swift and simple supper. The earthy, creamy beans work well with the herbs and wine. Prepared and cooked artichoke hearts are readily available, but if you are keen to use fresh artichokes, 3–4 large globe or 8–10 baby artichokes will yield roughly the right amount of flesh.

Heat the oil in a shallow saucepan or casserole. Add the shallot, celery and a pinch of salt and cook gently over medium-low heat for 10 minutes, until softened.

Add the garlic and cook for 2 minutes more, then add the wine. Turn the heat to medium-high and reduce by half.

Add the beans, stock, thyme and bay leaf. Reduce to a very gentle simmer and pop on the lid. Cook for 8 minutes, until the beans start to collapse. Meanwhile, put a pan of salted water on to boil for the pasta.

Stir the artichokes into the saucepan and cook for a final 5 minutes, until warmed through. Taste and tweak the seasoning with salt, pepper and a squeeze or 2 of lemon juice, if needed. Switch off the stove. Put the pasta in to boil (cook it according to the packet instructions) and leave the beans mixture to rest while the pasta cooks. If it seems a little thick, add a dash of pasta cooking water to it before you drain the pasta.

Drain the pasta and throw it into the pan of beans with a glug more olive oil. Transfer to bowls, garnish with the parsley and serve.

KOREAN STICKY MUSHROOMS WITH KIMCHI GREENS

SERVES 2

4 portobello mushrooms,
    thickly sliced
untoasted sesame oil
2 small pinches of salt
150g jasmine rice
½ tablespoon sesame seeds
1 head of pak choi, roughly sliced
150g tenderstem broccoli
80g kimchi, chopped
1 spring onion, very finely
    sliced, to garnish

For the sticky sauce
2cm piece of fresh root ginger,
    finely grated
1 garlic clove, finely chopped
2 tablespoons rice vinegar
2 tablespoons soy sauce
2 tablespoons agave nectar
1½ teaspoons Korean Gochujang
    chilli powder

Korean chilli powder is often available in supermarkets. Its smoky, toasted flavour gives a lovely warmth. The sauce has a good kick to it, but add less chilli powder if that's not your thing. If you're unfamiliar with kimchi, it is a spicy fermented cabbage, readily available in the UK. It is strongly flavoured and deeply savoury and is mostly used as a condiment. It gives the greens a delicious flavour boost in this dish.

Preheat the oven to 200°C (Gas Mark 6). Put a kettle on to boil.

Toss the mushrooms with some sesame oil and a small pinch of salt in a roasting tray. Roast for 15 minutes, until nicely browned.

Meanwhile, place the rice in a saucepan with a pinch of salt and cover with boiling water. Cook for 10–12 minutes until tender. Drain and set aside.

Meanwhile, mix together the sticky sauce ingredients.

Add the sauce to the browned mushrooms and mix well. Scatter with sesame seeds and return the roasting tray to the oven for a final 5 minutes, until sticky but not burnt.

Meanwhile, lightly steam or stir-fry the pak choi and broccoli until tender. Mix it with the chopped kimchi.

Serve the rice and greens in a bowl, topped with the sticky mushrooms. Garnish with the spring onions.

FOUR/FIVE/SIX~BEAN CHILLI

SERVES 8

1 tablespoon coconut oil
2 onions, chopped
3 celery sticks, chopped
250g mushrooms, chopped
5 garlic cloves, chopped
2 teaspoons chilli powder,
  or to taste
500g passata
1 can of plum tomatoes, squashed
½ tablespoon tomato purée
1 teaspoon balsamic vinegar
1 teaspoon ketchup
1 teaspoon sugar
400g can butter beans
400g can kidney beans
400g can black eyed beans
400g can borlotti beans
salt and pepper

This is my all-time favourite recipe. I loved it as a kid and I love it now. It goes with anything and works on top of rice, jacket potatoes, on its own, or in wraps, in every season, at home or when I'm on holiday, when I visit the moon... When I was a kid, every time my mother made this dish, I could smell it a mile away and could not wait to eat it. This is my vegan version. It has four different types of bean, but add as many types as you like!

Melt the coconut oil in a BIG pan. Add the onion and celery and fry over medium heat for about 10 minutes, until soft. Mix in the mushrooms, garlic and chilli powder and cook for 10 minutes. Now stir in the passata, canned tomatoes and the tomato purée and allow the mixture to heat up again after these additions.

While the sauce is coming to a simmer, combine the balsamic vinegar, ketchup and sugar in a small bowl or jug, then stir this mixture into the sauce. Drain the canned beans and add them all to the sauce, then season.

Put a lid on the saucepan and let the chilli slowly simmer for 30–40 minutes. (You can always add a little bit of veg stock to loosen the sauce if needed during this time.) Serve and enjoy.

DONER KEBABS WITH PINK PICKLE

MAKES 4

For the pink pickle
150ml cider vinegar
2 tablespoons brown sugar
1 bay leaf
¼ teaspoon caraway seeds
¼ teaspoon ground allspice
1 teaspoon salt
1 beetroot, peeled and cut
    into fine matchsticks
1 shallot, thinly sliced
½ fennel bulb, very thinly sliced
3 radishes, thinly sliced

For the kebab
sunflower or vegetable oil,
    for frying
350g Kebab Kofta Seitan Sausage
    (see page 145), cut into thin
    slices
small bunch of mint, chopped
200ml vegan yogurt
4 pitta breads
200g Pritchmmus Hummus
    (see page 172)
80g interesting mixed salad
    leaves
hot chilli sauce, to taste
2 tablespoons Dukkah
    (see page 161)

Best eaten on a kerbside at three in the morning, perhaps after having a bit too much to drink. Failing that, you'll still love this healthy, vegan version of a well-loved junk food classic! The pickle needs to be made in advance but can be used on the day of pickling. It mellows over time and can be stored in the fridge for up to 4 weeks, as long as the liquid covers the veg. You can tweak this recipe endlessly – try Babaganoush (see page 58) or Tahini Dressing (see page 71) instead of hummus, or some Crimson Kraut (see page 159) or Scandi Slaw (see page 160).

To make the pickle, heat the vinegar, sugar, bay leaf, spices and salt in a pan until dissolved. Pack the sliced veg into a sterilized 500ml clip-top jar. Pour in the warm liquid to the top. Close and leave for at least a few hours until cold, but preferably for a couple of days, if not weeks.

To make the kebabs, heat 2 tablespoons oil in a large frying pan, add the seitan and cook over a medium-high heat for 3–4 minutes, until nicely coloured and heated through.

While the seitan fries, mix the mint into the yogurt. Lightly toast the pittas and split them open along 1 side.

Slather some hummus inside each pitta and add a spoonful of drained pink pickles. Tuck in a small handful of salad leaves, followed by a generous serving of the fried seitan. Add a drizzle of yogurt and as much chilli sauce as you fancy. Finish with a scattering of dukkah. Eat with gusto.

FRIED TEMPEH SAMBAL and COCONUT RICE

SERVES 4

3 tablespoons vegetable oil
200g tempeh, cut into 2-cm dice
1 red pepper, deseeded and sliced
200g green beans, trimmed
100ml water
salt
bunch of coriander,
    chopped, to garnish

For the sambal paste
3 shallots
2 garlic cloves
4cm piece of galangal or
    fresh root ginger, peeled
2 ripe tomatoes
4 red bird's eye chillies
1½ tablespoons palm sugar
    (or use brown sugar)
1 tablespoon tamarind paste
1 tablespoon soy sauce

For the rice
400ml coconut milk
250ml water
pinch of salt
1 lemongrass stick, bashed to
    split it open but still intact
3 cardamom pods, split
1 teaspoon turmeric
250g jasmine rice, rinsed

Made from fermented and pressed soy beans, tempeh has a distinct savoury flavour and is high in protein. This is based on a popular, deep-fried Indonesian dish called Sambal Goreng. You can use any veg that stir-fries well.

To make the paste, blitz all the ingredients together in a small food processor or a pestle and mortar. Set aside.

To cook the rice, bring the coconut milk and measured water to a gentle simmer with the lemongrass, cardamon, turmeric and a pinch of salt. Stir in the rice. Cover and simmer over low heat for 10 minutes. Turn off the heat and leave for 6–8 minutes to steam and finish cooking, by which time all the liquid should have been absorbed.

While the rice cooks, heat the oil in a wok or large frying pan. Add the tempeh and fry over medium heat for 5–6 minutes, until golden brown. Remove with a slotted spoon and set aside.

Tip away some of the oil from the wok and add the pepper and beans. Stir-fry for 2 minutes, until beginning to soften, then add the sambal paste. Cook over medium heat for 3–4 minutes, stirring, until fragrant. Return the tempeh to the wok along with the measured water. Season with salt and cook for a further 5 minutes, until most of the liquid has evaporated and everything is cooked through.

Remove the lemongrass from the rice, stir through the coriander, and serve with the sambal.

GUEST CHEF: MR NICE PIE'S CREAMY MUSHROOM PIE

SERVES 2

For the filling
4 tablespoons rapeseed oil
250g good-quality mushrooms,
    preferably shiitake or
    chanterelle, chopped
    into bite-sized pieces
1 large onion, sliced
approximately 2 tablespoons
    plain flour
1 vegetable stock cube
50ml vegan sherry
100ml oat milk,
    plus extra to glaze
50ml oat cream
2 tablespoons lemon juice
approximately 2 tablespoons
    pepper
50g frozen petit pois

For the pastry
100g wholemeal flour,
    plus extra for dusting
pinch of salt
3–4 thyme leaves, broken
50g vegetable shortening,
    frozen and grated
2–3 teaspoons chilled water
pepper, to taste

From the brilliant vegan pie makers, this is rich and creamy with a wholesome, satisfying crumbly crust.

To make the filling, heat 3 tablespoons of the oil in a saucepan, add the mushrooms and fry over medium-low heat for 10–15 minutes or until golden, then set aside. Fry the onion and remaining oil in the same saucepan over medium-low heat for 5–10 minutes, until translucent. Mix in just enough plain flour to give a scrambled egg consistency.

Preheat the oven to 200°C (Gas Mark 6).

Crumble the stock cube into the saucepan, mix well and cook for a further 4–5 minutes. Now gradually whisk in the sherry and the oat milk until the consistency of a thick cream and allow the sherry to cook off for a couple of minutes. Str in the oat cream to thin the mixture a little, then add the lemon juice, black pepper and salt to taste. Finally, mix in the mushrooms and petit pois. Simmer for 3–5 minutes. Taste and adjust the seasoning if needed.

To make the pastry, add the flour, salt, pepper, thyme and shortening to a mixing bowl. Gently rub together with your fingers, then gradually mix in water to make a crumbly dough. Roll out the pastry to your desired thickness. Transfer the filling to a large pie tin and place the pastry lid on top, crimping the edges to seal. Glaze with a little oat milk. Make a little hole in the centre of the lid to allow steam to escape. Bake for 40 minutes, until the pastry is golden brown.

PRITCHARD PAELLA
SERVES 6

1.4 litres vegetable stock,
   plus extra as required
75cl bottle of dry white
   wine (something like
   a Chardonnay)
pinch of saffron threads
500g paella rice
2 tablespoons olive oil
2 onions, chopped
3 peppers (of any colour),
   roughly chopped
4 garlic cloves, crushed
½ tablespoon cayenne pepper,
   or more to taste
1 tablespoon paprika
8 small tomatoes, halved
100g green beans, chopped
1 × 350g Chorizo Seitan Sausage
   (see page 145), sliced
150g tofu, crumbled
salt
pepper

To garnish
2 limes, sliced
a pinch of nutritional yeast
2 tablespoons crispy seaweed
   flakes, for sprinkling

During the filming of the TV series, we wanted to convince a ladies' rugby team that vegan food isn't boring. This seafood-free paella with vegan chorizo was the dish chosen to win them over and, I'm telling you, it went down a storm!

Preheat the oven to 180°C (Gas Mark 4).

Pour the stock and wine into a large saucepan and stir in the saffron. Bring to a slow boil. Add the rice, reduce the heat and simmer for 15 minutes. Keep an eye on the rice and don't stir it too much. If it starts to boil dry, add more stock.

Meanwhile, heat a little oil in a large paella pan. Add the onion and peppers with a sprinkling of salt and cook over medium heat for 5 minutes, until beginning to soften. Add the garlic and spices and cook for another 10 minutes.

Once the rice has absorbed most – but not all – of the liquid in the saucepan, transfer it to the paella pan. Stir to combine all of the ingredients, then mix in the tomatoes and green beans. If the mixture seems too dry, add some more stock at this stage. Transfer the paella pan into the oven and bake for 30 minutes.

Heat the remaining oil in a frying pan. Add the seitan sausage and tofu and cook over medium-high heat for 3–4 minutes until brown and crispy.

Remove the paella from the oven and add the tofu and seitan sausage to the dish. Combine gently. Serve immediately in the paella pan, garnished with slices of lime, nutritional yeast and a sprinkling of crispy seaweed for that wow factor.

 GREEN LENTIL COTTAGE PIE

SERVES 4

1kg potatoes, peeled,
   quartered if large
1 tablespoon rapeseed oil
1 red onion, chopped into
   chunky pieces
1 courgette, chopped into
   chunky pieces
4 carrots, chopped into
   chunky pieces
3 red peppers, chopped into
   chunky pieces
2 fresh tomatoes,
   roughly chopped
500ml vegetable stock
400g can chopped tomatoes
1 tablespoon tomato purée
200g green lentils, rinsed
1 teaspoon smoked paprika,
   plus extra to serve
2 bay leaves
3 tablespoons dairy-free spread
6 tablespoons dairy-free milk
salt

Packed with protein, thanks to the lentils. As a youngster I always linked lentils with hippies, but now I'm older I'm cooking with the blasted things (lentils, not hippies). Don't use canned lentils for this – soaked dried ones make for a much better pie.

Preheat the oven to 200°C (Gas Mark 6).

Put the potatoes into a saucepan of water and bring to a boil. Boil for 15–20 minutes, until tender.

Meanwhile, heat the oil in a saucepan over medium heat, add the chopped veg, except for the tomatoes, and sweat for around 5 minutes. Season the veg, add the fresh tomatoes, give it a stir and cook for another 10 minutes, until soft.

Pour the stock into the saucepan, then mix in the canned tomatoes, tomato purée and 150ml water. Stir in the lentils, then simmer for 20 minutes until the lentils are almost tender. Add the smoked paprika and bay leaves and stir.

Once the potatoes are ready, drain well, then return them to the pan, add the dairy-free spread and milk and mash.

Once the green lentils have grown in size and have absorbed some of the liquid, transfer the mixture to an ovenproof dish. Pipe or spoon over your potato – be careful as it will be hot – and finish with a sprinkling of smoked paprika. Transfer the dish to the oven and bake for 20 minutes or so, until the potato is golden on top.

SICILIAN CAULIFLOWER WITH FARINATA

SERVES 4

For the farinata
150g chickpea flour
450ml warm water
½ teaspoon salt
2 tablespoons olive oil

For the cauliflower
1 cauliflower, cut into
    bite-sized florets
olive oil
3 shallots, sliced
4 celery sticks, sliced
1 tablespoon tomato purée
2 teaspoons soft brown sugar
2 garlic cloves, chopped
3 tablespoons red wine vinegar
pinch of saffron threads, soaked
    in 2 tablespoons hot water
400g ripe tomatoes, chopped
80g pitted black olives, halved
40g sultanas
2 tablespoons capers, chopped
40g pine nuts, toasted
small bunch of basil
salt and pepper

This dish is best served warm or at room temperature. The tomatoes are warmed gently – you don't want them to cook down into a sauce. Instead, let the mixture rest to allow all the favours to mingle and mature. If you have the chance or are planning ahead, let it sit for two or three hours and gently reheat it before serving. The farinata batter is all the better for a long rest, too. Farinata is a chickpea flour pancake that is perfect alongside rich veg dishes. It adds a bit of protein and mops up all the flavoursome sauce at the end. The batter looks worryingly thin, but don't panic, it will thicken and set under the grill.

Preheat the oven to 200°C (Gas Mark 6).

First, make the farinata batter. Put the flour into a mixing bowl. Slowly whisk the measured water into the flour until you have a smooth, thin batter. Whisk in the salt and olive oil. Leave to rest for at least 30 minutes.

Meanwhile, place the cauliflower florets in a roasting tray. Oil them well, then season with salt and pepper. Roast for 12–15 minutes, until nicely coloured and tender.

Warm some olive oil in a wide saucepan. Add the shallots and celery and fry gently over medium-low heat for 10 minutes, until starting to soften. Mix in the tomato purée, sugar, garlic, vinegar and saffron and water. Cook for another 2–3 minutes, until the sugar has dissolved.

Recipe continued overleaf

Recipe continued

Now tip in the cauliflower, tomatoes, olives, sultanas and capers. Mix together, then warm gently for 3 minutes. Remove from the heat and adjust the seasoning to taste. Leave to rest while you make the farinata.

Heat your grill on a medium-high setting. Heat a layer of olive oil in a large heatproof non-stick frying pan over medium heat. Tip in the rested farinata batter and cook it for 4–5 minutes, until the underside begins to set. Slide the frying pan under the grill and cook for a further 3–4 minutes, until fully set, coloured and crisp on top. Leave to rest for a few minutes, then turn out onto a board.

Add the pine nuts to the cauliflower, tear in the basil and mix together. Slice or tear the farinata into generous pieces and serve alongside the warm cauliflower.

CELERIAC STEAKS and RED WINE LENTILS

SERVES 4

600ml boiling water
20g dried porcini mushrooms
1 large celeriac
2 tablespoons olive oil,
    plus extra for frying
3 shallots, diced
2 celery sticks, diced
1 carrot, diced
250g Puy or beluga lentils
1 bay leaf
175ml red wine
½ tablespoon Dijon mustard
salt and pepper
handful of flat-leaf parsley,
    torn, to serve
greens of your choice, to serve

For the sauce
60g toasted walnuts
1 tablespoon capers
1 garlic clove, chopped
1 tablespoon chopped rosemary
2 tablespoons lemon juice,
    to taste
6 tablespoons olive oil
salt and pepper

I call these 'steaks' for want of a better word. They are being fried and sliced in the same way as their meat counterparts, and you get to enjoy a nice chunk of succulent, juicy celeriac flesh with gusto. Using dried mushrooms makes for a dark, flavourful stock that adds depth to this delicious dish. Serve with kale, spinach or chard, cooked in your favourite way.

Put a pan of water on to boil for your celeriac.

Pour the measured boiling water into a bowl. Add the dried mushrooms to the water and leave to soak.

Meanwhile, peel the celeriac and slice it horizontally into 4 equally thick slices. These are your steaks. Season them well, then poach or steam them for 15–20 minutes, until they are easily pierced with a knife. Remove from the pan and set aside.

While the celeriac cooks, warm 2 tablespoons olive oil in a saucepan and gently fry the shallot, celery and carrot over medium-low heat for 5 minutes, until they begin to soften.

Add the lentils, bay leaf and wine to the saucepan. Cook for 3–4 minutes while the wine bubbles away and reduces by half, then tip in the liquid from the mushrooms. Roughly chop the rehydrated mushrooms and add those to the pan, too. Bring the mixture to a very gentle simmer and cook, loosely covered, for 25–30 minutes, until the lentils are

Recipe continued overleaf

Recipe continued

tender but not mushy. Most of the liquid should have been absorbed. Add a dash more water if they dry out before they are cooked.

While the lentils are cooking, make the sauce. Put the walnuts, capers, garlic and rosemary into a mini food processor or a pestle and mortar and blend together with enough olive oil to give you a thick pesto-like consistency (you may need to add 1–2 tablespoons of water). Season with salt, pepper and lemon juice to taste. Set aside.

To fry the celeriac steaks, warm 2 tablespoons olive oil in a frying pan, add the steaks and fry for 4–5 minutes per side until golden brown. Finish them with plenty of black pepper.

When the lentils are done, stir in the mustard and season with salt and pepper to taste, then transfer to serving plates. Slice each steak thickly and sit the slices on top of a portion of lentils. Spoon a little of the sauce over the top. Sprinkle with parsley and serve with the greens of your choice.

GUEST CHEF: ONE PLANET PIZZA DOUGH

MAKES 4

For the dough (to make 4 medium pizzas)
560g strong white bread flour, sifted, plus extra for dusting
1 teaspoon freshly ground salt
7g fast-action dried yeast
½ teaspoon ground flax seeds
2 tablespoons rapeseed oil (ideally cold-pressed)
240ml water (preferably filtered) mixed with 100ml boiling water (also preferably filtered)

For the sauce
400g can chopped tomatoes (ideally organic)
3 garlic cloves
2 teaspoons chia seeds
1 teaspoon dried basil
1 teaspoon dried oregano
½ teaspoon freshly ground salt

These guys didn't get crowdfunded into business for nothing, they really know a thing or two about putting together a good pizza. You won't believe how easy it is to make a delicious vegan pizza at home. Just follow their guidance below (you can dough this!). All you have to do is think about your toppings (moo've over dairy!), with some help from the following pages. One Planet use Bute Island's Sheese and/or any fruit and veg of your choice (yes, that includes pineapple!). (Puns courtesy of One Planet. Don't blame me.)

Add the flour, salt, yeast and flax seeds into a large mixing bowl. Stir the oil into your (now lukewarm) measured water.

Pour the liquid into the flour mix. Use your hands to mix and knead into a soft dough that doesn't stick to the side of the bowl. Cover the bowl with a damp tea towel and leave in a warm place for approximately 1 hour, until doubled in size.

Preheat the oven to 250°C (Gas Mark 9).

Split your dough into 2 balls. Knead for up to 2 minutes on a floured surface, then stretch or roll it out to the desired size. Transfer each to a baking sheet and part-cook for 3 minutes.

Blitz the sauce ingredients in a blender until smooth.

When the part-cooking time has elapsed, remove your bases from the oven and smear over the sauce. Add the toppings of your choice. Return to the oven and cook for a further 10 minutes, until fully cooked. Serve straight away.

SPICED TURKISH LENTIL PIZZA

MAKES 2

400g can cooked puy
  lentils, drained
1 garlic clove, finely chopped
1 tablespoon harissa
30g sultanas, chopped
1 teaspoon ground cumin
1 teaspoon smoked paprika
½ teaspoon ground cinnamon
½ teaspoon dried oregano
2 tablespoons olive oil
One Planet Pizza Dough
  and sauce (see opposite)
1 quantity Tahini Dressing
  (see page 71)
40g pine nuts, toasted
½ small shallot or red onion,
  very finely sliced
small bunch of mint, chopped
small bunch of flat-leaf or
  curly parsley, chopped
salt and pepper

This topping idea is based on a traditional Turkish spiced flatbread, but using lentils instead of minced lamb. The lentils should crisp up a little at the edges as they cook.

In a large bowl, mix together the lentils, garlic, harissa, sultanas, spices and olive oil. Season with salt and pepper.

Once you've spread a very thin layer of tomato sauce on each pizza base (see opposite), divide the lentil mixture into 2 equal portions and use each portion to top 1 pizza, scattering it as evenly as you can. Bake as directed opposite.

When the pizzas are ready, artistically streak them with some tahini dressing. Scatter over the pine nuts, red onion and herbs. Cut into fat wedges and serve.

Pictured overleaf

POTATO and ROSEMARY PIZZA

MAKES 2

250g small new or salad
  potatoes, very finely sliced
  with a mandoline
150g asparagus, trimmed
  and thinly sliced
2 sprigs of rosemary,
  roughly chopped
2 tablespoons olive oil
One Planet Pizza Dough
  and sauce (see opposite)
50g vegan Parmesan
  cheese, grated
salt and pepper

For this topping, the potatoes need to be cut wafer thin, which is best done with a mandoline, but a very sharp knife will do. It may seem like there are too few potatoes, but once you've sliced them you'll see that a little will go a long way. Everything gets tossed in olive oil so that it roasts nicely in the oven instead of scorching.

Put the potatoes, asparagus and rosemary into a bowl, add the olive oil and mix well. Season well with salt and black pepper.

Once you've spread a very thin layer of tomato sauce on each pizza base (see page 136), divide the potato mixture into 2 equal portions and use each portion to top 1 pizza, spreading it as evenly as you can. Bake as directed on page 136.

Grate over the Parmesan as soon as the pizzas come out of the oven. Cut into fat wedges and serve immediately.

Pictured on pages 138-9

CHILLI SQUASH, SPINACH and MUSHROOM PIZZA

MAKES 2

400g squash, cut into
    2-cm chunks
olive oil
150g spinach
2 portobello mushrooms,
    thinly sliced
One Planet Pizza Dough and
    sauce (see opposite)
½ small red onion, sliced
150g vegan mozzarella,
    grated or torn
dried smoked chilli flakes
salt and pepper

A great flavour combination! But you need to do a bit of work to get it, because the spinach and mushrooms must be cooked before using them to top the pizza bases. They both release so much liquid as they cook, they'd make the whole thing too soggy if they were cooked on the base. But cooking them first works brilliantly, so it's totally worth the effort.

Preheat the oven to 200°C (Gas Mark 6). Put a pan of water on to boil.

Put the squash chunks into a roasting tray, add enough oil to cover and toss to coat them well in the oil. Season with salt and pepper. Roast for 25 minutes, until tender.

Meanwhile, blanch the spinach in the saucepan of boiling water for 30 seconds, until wilted. Drain and cool immediately in cold water. Drain the spinach once again, then squeeze out the excess water. Roughly chop the spinach and set aside.

Lightly cover the base of a frying pan with oil and heat it up. Add the mushrooms, season with salt and fry over medium-low heat for 5 minutes, until they have darkened and released most of their water.

Once you've spread a very thin layer of tomato sauce on each pizza base (see page 136), scatter over half the onions, spinach, mushrooms and squash. Top with the mozzarella and a pinch or 2 of chilli flakes. Bake as directed on page 136. Cut into fat wedges and serve.

Pictured on pages 138–9

DIRTY VEGAN SEITAN

MAKES 700G

For the seitan
230g vital wheat gluten
30g nutritional yeast flakes
2 tablespoons plain flour
1 tablespoon olive oil
250ml vegetable stock
or water

For the poaching stock
1 large garlic clove
2.5 litres cold vegetable stock
1 tablespoon tomato purée
120ml soy sauce

For the coating
vegetable oil, for deep-frying
250g rice crumbs

I can't believe that something that is not actually meat tastes so much like it. I tasted a seitan chicken nugget and honestly thought I was eating the real thing. Vital wheat gluten is available online and this version tastes amazing (though if you are gluten intolerant, then this is a no-no!)

Mix the vital wheat gluten, nutritional yeast, flour and olive oil in a bowl. Slowly add the stock or water and combine with your hands until you have a dough ball. Knead the dough for 4–5 minutes or until it is easy to handle and elastic. Now divide it into 4 equal chunks.

Stir together the poaching stock ingredients in a pan and place the seitan carefully in the stock. Put a lid on the pan. Bring the poaching stock to a boil, then reduce the heat to medium-low and simmer for 30 minutes. Now turn the seitan chunks over in the pan and cook for another 20 minutes. Ensure the seitan is covered in liquid throughout cooking. Remove the pan from the heat and leave the seitan cool in the stock. Once cooled, cut it into bite-sized chunks, ready for coating.

Pour enough vegetable oil into a medium saucepan for deep-frying and heat it up.

Put the rice crumbs into a shallow bowl with a bowl of water next to it. Dip each seitan chunk in the water, then roll in the rice crumbs. (If they don't stick, mix a little plain flour into the water.) Lower the coated seitan into the hot oil and cook for 2 minutes, until golden. Drain on kitchen paper and use as a meat substitute with dips, in curries, kebabs or fry-ups.

SEITAN SAUSAGES

MAKES 700G

CHORIZO SAUSAGES

230g vital wheat gluten
30g nutritional yeast flakes
2 tablespoons plain flour
1 tablespoon smoked paprika
2 tablespoons paprika
1 teaspoon dried oregano
½ teaspoon ground fennel seeds
1 garlic clove, finely chopped
1 teaspoon salt
pinch of cayenne pepper
280ml vegetable stock
100ml dry sherry
2 tablespoons soy sauce
1 tablespoon tomato purée
2 tablespoons olive oil

ENGLISH BREAKFAST SAUSAGES

230g vital wheat gluten
30g nutritional yeast flakes
2 tablespoons plain flour
½ tablespoon dried sage
1 teaspoon dried thyme
good pinch of white pepper
good pinch of nutmeg
good pinch of allspice
1 garlic clove, finely chopped
1 teaspoon salt
320ml mushroom stock (steep
    a handful of dried porcini
    mushrooms in 350ml boiling
    water, leave to cool, then strain
    and use the liquid as stock)
2 tablespoons vegan
    Worcestershire sauce
2 tablespoons cider vinegar
1 tablespoon tomato purée
2 tablespoons olive oil

When fried, seitan has a similar texture to meat that can be put to good use in the vegan kitchen. Think kebabs (see page 120), paella (see page 126) and sausages in your full breakfast. With this recipe, you can make two large 350g sausages that can be sliced and fried. They will keep well in an airtight container in the fridge for four or five days. And they freeze well (for up to 3 months), so it makes sense to make two, use one fresh and pop one in the freezer for a later date. Here I provide three flavour variations for different occasions. Feel free to make up your own – as long as the liquid-to-dry ratios remain the same, you can adapt and tweak the flavours to your tastes. When ready to cook, simply slice up the sausage and fry the slices in a little oil over medium-high heat for 3 minutes on each side, until coloured and crispy at the edges.

Mix all the dry ingredients together in a bowl. Add the wet ingredients and knead together, as if making bread, for 5 minutes, until you have a firm dough.

Divide the mixture into 2 equal portions. Form each half into a rough log shape. Lay out a sheet of clingfilm and place 1 log in the centre. Roll the clingfilm around the log, push out any trapped air and twist the ends of the clingfilm together around the log to tighten it into a large sausage shape. This is best done by holding the clingfilm ends and rolling the log along the work surface a few times until the

Recipe continued overleaf

KEBAB KOFTA SAUSAGES

230g vital wheat gluten

30g nutritional yeast flakes

2 tablespoons plain flour

2 teaspoons ground cumin

1 teaspoon ground coriander

½ teaspoon ground cinnamon

1 garlic clove, finely chopped

few turns of black pepper

1 teaspoon salt

320ml vegetable stock

2 tablespoons soy sauce

2 tablespoons cider vinegar

2 tablespoons harissa paste

2 tablespoons olive oil

Recipe continued

clingfilm is drum-skin tight. Now wrap it neatly in kitchen foil. Repeat the rolling process with the other half.

Place the wrapped sausages in a large saucepan of water and bring it up to a low simmer. Poach the sausages gently over low heat for 1 hour, topping up the water if necessary, until they feel very firm when squeezed.

Remove the logs from the water and leave to cool, then pop them in the fridge to chill overnight. Don't remove the wrapping until they are completely chilled, or they will expand and lose their shape.

VEGETABLE CASSEROLE

SERVES 4

olive oil
1 onion, finely chopped
2 celery sticks, finely chopped
3 garlic cloves, finely chopped
2 courgettes, chopped
2 carrots, chopped
½ swede, chopped
250g mushrooms, chopped
500ml bottle of vegan ale
500ml vegetable stock
1 leek, finely chopped
150g pearl barley
200g canned chopped tomatoes
1 sprig of rosemary
2 teaspoons dried sage
bread or mashed potato,
    to serve (optional)

A rooty veg winter warmer, and one for the end of a long day. Once you've assembled all your veg in a casserole and given them a quick fry, add the ale and stock, then just chuck the dish in the oven and leave it to cook. Sit down with a glass of wine and, an hour and half later, you're feasting. Make sure you have some nice bread to mop up what sauce is left.

Preheat the oven to 200°C (Gas Mark 6).

Heat the oil in a casserole. Add the onion, celery, garlic, courgette, carrot, swede and mushrooms and fry for about 10–15 minutes, until soft.

Stir the ale and stock into the casserole, then add the leeks, pearl barley, canned tomato, sprig of rosemary and sage and stir well. Put the lid on the casserole and transfer to the oven. Cook for 1½ hours, until all the veg is cooked. Serve on its own or with bread or mashed potato.

PRITCHARD'S DIRTY VEGAN BURGER

· MAKES 4 ·

vegetable or sunflower oil,
   for frying, plus extra for
   deep-frying
1 medium onion
30g garlic cloves
2 teaspoons turmeric
2 tablespoons mild curry powder
1 teaspoon chilli powder
1 teaspoon cayenne pepper
100g cauliflower, cut into
   medium pieces
1 small Scotch bonnet chilli,
   deseeded if preferred
2 × 400g cans of chickpeas,
   drained
3 teaspoons Dijon mustard
25g coriander, roughly chopped
pinch of salt
pinch of cracked black pepper
juice of 1 lime
150g oats

To serve
4 bread rolls, split
hot chilli sauce
mango chutney
crisp lettuce leaves
vegan tzatziki
Aioli (see page 45)
4 fat slices of beef tomato
red onion, sliced into
   12 thin rings

If you have the urgent need for a vegan burger and happen to be in Cardiff, The Grazing Shed is the place to head for. They know how to turn fresh, local produce into the type of vegan burger you might almost kill for. I hooked up with their chef Adam Walker to create this recipe – a curry burger with a kick of heat and some mango chutney cutting through it. A naughty vegan treat. To maximize the luxury factor, use high-quality ingredients, paying particular attention to the type of bread you choose – it is paramount to the enjoyment. And remember that the build of the PDVB is important, so follow my instructions to the letter! All the flavours complement each other and lead the lucky eater on a journey of spice, salt, sweet and freshness.

Heat a little oil in a frying pan and add the onion, garlic and dried spices. Fry over a medium heat for a few minutes, then add the cauliflower pieces and fry for 5 more minutes, to allow the cauliflower to soften.

Transfer the mixture into the bowl of a food processor with the Scotch bonnet and combine until finely chopped. (Alternatively, chop everything finely and combine in a bowl.)

Transfer the mixture to a bowl and combine by hand, mixing thoroughly.

Using a blender, potato masher or your hands, smash up the chickpeas until smooth. Add to the mixture in the bowl with the mustard and combine by hand until the mixture is well blended and holds together. At this point the texture will be quite wet. Mix in the coriander, salt, pepper and lime juice. Now slowly incorporate the oats until the mixture begins to stiffen and becomes tacky rather than sticky. Divide the mixture into 4 equal portions and shape each of these into a patty.

Heat your oil ready for deep-frying. You don't want to cook the patties at a super-high temperature. If you have a cooking thermometer, aim for 170°C. Deep-fry the patties for 3 minutes or until golden brown and crisp on the outside, and hot and fluffy on the inside. Remove carefully with a slotted spoon and drain on a plate lined with kitchen paper.

To build each burger, take the top bun and make a circle of hot chilli sauce towards the outside edge of the cut surface. Fill the circle with mango chutney. Repeat on the lower bun. Now place 1 patty on the lower bun. Add a zig zag of aioli directly to the patty, then place a juicy slice of beef tomato on top. Fill a leaf with tzatziki, then lovingly place it over the tomato. Top with 3 thinly sliced rings of fresh red onion. Add the top bun, ensuring you do not squash the ingredients together too much. Enjoy.

Pictured overleaf

SUMMER PILAF

SERVES 4

3 tablespoons olive oil
1 onion, finely diced
300g white basmati rice, rinsed
4 long strips of lemon zest (use
    a vegetable peeler to cut these)
1 small cinnamon stick
pinch of saffron threads
3 cardamom pods, split
1 bay leaf
6 tablespoons water
200g asparagus, steamed
    and sliced
150g cooked and skinned
    broad beans
100g peas, defrosted
small bunch of dill, chopped
40g flaked and toasted almonds
lemon juice, to taste
salt and pepper

There are plenty of pilaf recipes that just add stuff to rice and cook it to a mush. For a satisfying dish, you need to give the rice a bit of attention but the payoff is light, fragrant rice with well separated, fluffy grains. Switch the veg according to the seasons, or use up whatever's left over from a weekly local veggie box delivery! I'd recommend roasted root veg and chopped dried fruit for a winter version.

Heat 1 tablespoon of the olive oil in a large saucepan. Add the onion and cook over low heat for 10 minutes.

Simmer the rice in a pan of well-salted, boiling water for 5 minutes. Drain well and season it with salt. Set aside.

Add the zest, cinnamon, saffron, cardamom, bay leaf and the remaining olive oil to the onion. Fry gently for 1 minute. Add the measured water and gently fold in the rice. Level it out with a wooden spoon, trying not to compress it too much. Poke 12 holes into the rice with the spoon handle, pushing it down to the base of the pan – this allows steam to move through the rice. Stretch a tea towel across the top of the pan and place the lid firmly on top. Fold the edges and corners of the tea towel up and over the lid so they don't catch alight! Reduce the heat to the lowest setting and cook for 20 minutes, until the rice is tender, light and fluffy and just beginning to catch on the bottom of the pan.

Take the pan off the heat and mix in the green veg. Pop the lid back on and leave for 5 minutes to warm through. Fold through the dill and almonds. Taste and tweak the seasoning with salt, pepper and lemon juice if needed.

VEGAN SAUSAGE CASSEROLE
SERVES 4

8 vegan sausages
½ tablespoon coconut oil
1 large onion, diced
4 garlic cloves, chopped
4 carrots, sliced or diced
4 tomatoes, quartered
400g can chopped tomatoes
1 tablespoon tomato purée
200ml vegetable stock
½ teaspoon smoked paprika
1 sprig of thyme, plus extra,
    fresh growing thyme,
    to garnish
400g can borlotti beans
boiled new potatoes, to serve

....

I believe in cooking from scratch as much as possible, but now and then, a processed veggie sausage is your friend. Use your favourite brand – the sausages soak up the scrummy casserole juices nicely. (I've never used that word scrummy in my life, but it sums this up perfectly!) Hearty fare, vegan style.

....

Preheat the oven to 180°C (Gas Mark 4).

Cook your vegan sausages according to the packet instructions. (While they are cooking you can prep your ingredients.)

Heat the oil in a casserole. Add your diced onion and fry over medium-low heat for 5–10 minutes, until soft and golden. Add the garlic, carrot, fresh and canned tomatoes and tomato purée, the veg stock, paprika and thyme and stir all the ingredients together well. Bring the cooked sausages out of the oven and cut them into bite-sized pieces. Add these to the casserole, too.

Place a lid on the casserole and transfer to the oven. Cook for 15 minutes, then stir in the borlotti beans, replace the lid and return to the oven. Cook for another 15 minutes, until everything is cooked through and your house smells amazing! Serve with some boiled new potatoes.

THE MAIN'S BEST MATE

This is the stuff on the side – veggies
and sauces to spice up any meal.

RED CABBAGE and BEETS THREE WAYS

★

CRIMSON KRAUT

MAKES 500ML

375g finely shredded red
   cabbage, with one large
   whole leaf reserved
125g peeled and grated beetroot
12g fine sea salt
¼ teaspoon caraway seeds
6 juniper berries
1 bay leaf

This unlikely combination really works. The earthy flavours and bright colours of the veg complement each other, and they are both able to carry strong spicing and acidity.

Put the cabbage and beetroot in a large bowl. Add the salt and massage it into the veg for 5–10 minutes. The cabbage should become quite wet. Mix in the caraway seeds, juniper berries and bay leaf.

Pack tightly into a sterilized 500ml clip-top jar and place the whole cabbage leaf on top. The released liquid should cover the cabbage leaf completely. (If there's not enough liquid make a 2 per cent brine and add enough to cover.)

Leave at room temperature in a dark corner to ferment, opening the lid daily to release some of the gas during the first week. It's ready to eat after 1–2 weeks, but can be left a little longer to develop. It should be salty and savoury with a slight fizz, although some people take it to a point where it becomes almost sour and slightly farty.

When ready, remove the cabbage leaf and store the jar in the fridge until needed. It should keep for about 1 month.

SLOW *and* SPICED

SERVES 6~8

1 small red cabbage, finely sliced
1 beetroot, peeled and grated
1 large red onion, finely sliced
1 pear, peeled and grated
2 tablespoons soft brown sugar
1 small cinnamon stick
1 star anise
1 teaspoon allspice
1 bay leaf
125ml red wine
100ml water or vegetable stock
salt and pepper

Warm, fragrant and spicy – this is like Christmas in a bowl.

Mix everything in a heavy-based saucepan and season with salt and pepper. Pop on a lid and cook over low heat (or in a low oven, if you prefer) for about 1 hour, until soft, dark, sweet and spicy. Taste and tweak the seasoning as desired.

Pictured on page 158

★ PREP: 10 MINUTES ★

SCANDI SLAW

SERVES 4~6

2 good handfuls of finely
   shredded red cabbage
1 beetroot, peeled and cut
   into small matchsticks
1 apple, cored and diced
1 celery stick, finely diced
40g dried cranberries, chopped
30g chopped and toasted
   hazelnuts
2 tablespoons olive oil
1 tablespoon red wine vinegar
½ tablespoon Dijon mustard
small bunch of dill, chopped
pinch of allspice

A dollop of vegan yogurt wouldn't go amiss in the mix, too, as long as the flavour isn't too coconutty.

Mix everything together thoroughly and season with salt and pepper to taste.

Pictured on page 158

ROAST BROCCOLI and DUKKAH

SERVES 4

400g purple sprouting
   or tenderstem broccoli
olive oil
salt and pepper

For the dukkah
70g toasted hazelnuts
30g toasted pumpkin seeds
30g toasted sunflower seeds
20g toasted sesame seeds
1 tablespoon cumin seeds
1 tablespoon coriander seeds
½ tablespoon dried thyme
½ tablespoon sumac
½ teaspoon salt

Dukkah with roasted broccoli is a great combination, which isn't difficult because dukkah goes with just about anything. Lucky for you, this recipe will give you more dukkah than you need for four helpings, but the extra will keep for a month if stored at room temperature in a screw-top jar. Try it scattered across any roasted veg. This dish is perfect served with some Tahini Dressing (see page 71).

Preheat the oven to 200°C (Gas Mark 6).

To make the dukkah, put everything into a blender and pulse to a coarse breadcrumb-like texture. You want a nutty, seedy rubble – make sure you don't pulse it to a powder. (Alternatively, you can bash it all in a pestle and mortar.)

Trim the broccoli down into long spears of equal width. Place them in a roasting tray and season with salt and pepper. Add a little oil and toss to coat. Roast for 8–10 minutes, until the florets have started to colour and the stalks are tender.

Transfer the broccoli to a serving plate, scatter over a few tablespoons of dukkah and serve.

LEEKS & RUNNER BEANS WITH LEMON CAPERS

SERVES 4

4 leeks
16 runner beans, trimmed
and stringy edges removed
with a vegetable peeler
2 tablespoons capers, chopped
glug of olive oil
lemon juice, to taste
salt and pepper
small bunch of mint, chopped,
to garnish

This is the perfect dish for cooking on the barbecue, but a griddle pan works well, too. The beans should be blistered on the outside and just cooked on the inside.

Put a pan of salted water on to boil. Put a heavy griddle pan on the hob to get very hot, 10 minutes at least.

Poach the leeks in the boiling water for about 6 minutes, until they are easily pierced with a knife tip. Remove them from the pan and leave until cool enough to handle. Then peel away the soggy outer layer from the leeks and split them in half lengthways.

When the griddle pan is very hot, lay the leek halves on the griddle and cook for just under 1 minute on each side – just enough to char mark them, but not so much that they start to burn. Transfer to a plate and set aside.

Reduce the heat under the griddle pan a bit. Place the beans directly on the griddle and cook for 2–3 minutes per side until marked and blistered. Transfer to a chopping board.

Slice the leeks and beans into chunky pieces. Mix them together in a bowl with the capers, a glug of olive oil and a good squeeze of lemon juice. Season with salt and pepper and leave for at least 10 minutes before serving. Garnish with some freshly chopped mint when you do serve.

BROAD BEANS, FENNEL and CHERRY TOMATOES

SERVES 2

200g podded broad beans
   (600g in their pods)
2 tablespoons olive oil
1 large fennel bulb, thinly sliced
pinch of salt, plus extra to taste
200g cherry tomatoes
175ml white wine
1 garlic clove, finely chopped
few sprigs of oregano
   or marjoram

Summer veg in a lovely sauce – you can't go wrong with this one. Mix it with pasta, white beans or quinoa to turn it into a full meal.

Place the broad beans in a heatproof bowl and cover them with boiling water. Leave for 8–10 minutes, until the skins can be easily removed. Drain the beans and take a few minutes to slip the skins away from the beans. Set aside.

Warm the olive oil in a frying pan. Add the fennel with a pinch of salt and lightly fry over medium-low heat for 6–8 minutes, until it starts to colour.

Add the tomatoes to the pan and cook for 3–4 minutes, until they begin to soften, split and release a little liquid. Chuck in the white wine and garlic and mix well. Let the mixture bubble away for about 3 minutes, until reduced by half.

Throw in the broad beans and herbs. Gently warm them through for 2 minutes. Taste and tweak the seasoning. Serve immediately.

TRI-KALE

★

This is the ultimate kale dish – three different ways with kale, combined in one superlative side dish. It's riot of textures! You can serve each of these separately, but they work amazingly well when combined. To bring them together, fold the whipped kale into the wilted kale in the pan and let it warm through. Remove from the heat and fold in half the crispy kale. Pile into a serving dish and top with the remaining crispy stuff.

PREP: 5 MINUTES ★ COOK: 8–10 MINUTES

CRISPY KALE

200g curly kale,
  tough stems removed
2 tablespoons sunflower
  or vegetable oil
pinch of salt

Kale takes on a savoury, seaweed-like taste when roasted. If you can, turn off the fan in your oven, as it tends to blow the kale off the tray as it dries out. All ovens differ, so keep an eye on the kale so it doesn't burn.

Preheat the oven 190°C (Gas Mark 5).

Strip away and discard any large, tough-looking stalks. Tear the leaves into bite-sized pieces.

Put the kale into a bowl with the oil and a pinch of salt and mix together. Spread it all out on a baking tray. Transfer to the oven and roast for 8–10 minutes, turning once midway through, until crispy and starting to colour.

WHIPPED KALE

SERVES 2

200g curly kale,
   tough stems removed
Dijon mustard
olive oil
salt

....

This simple dish tastes like so much more than the sum of its parts. I haven't given strict quantities here as such, because it is mostly done to taste. You want a flavoursome purée which acts almost like a dressing.

....

Blanch the kale in boiling water for 3 minutes, until the stems have softened. Remove and cool immediately in cold water. Drain well and transfer to a blender.

Add a blob of mustard, a glug of olive oil and a good pinch of salt – all to taste – and whizz it all together. The whipped kale will keep in an airtight container in the fridge for a few days but loses its vibrant colour over time.

Pictured on page 166

WILTED KALE

SERVES 2

olive oil
200g curly kale,
   tough stems removed
1 garlic clove, finely chopped
pinch of salt
lemon juice, to taste

....

Simple and effective, this dish lets the flavour of the kale do its thing. Avoid drying the kale after washing it. The residual water on the leaves helps them to wilt more quickly in the pan.

....

Warm a little oil in a saucepan. Add the kale and cook gently for 2 minutes, until starting to wilt. Add the garlic and cook for a further 2 minutes until tender. Season with a pinch of salt and finish with a squeeze or two of lemon.

Pictured on page 166

ORANGE, MISO and SESAME ROASTED CARROTS

MAKES 4

500g carrots
2 tablespoons sesame oil
    (untoasted)
juice of ½ orange
2 tablespoons sweet white miso
salt

To garnish
1 tablespoon toasted
    sesame seeds
small bunch of coriander

Carrot and orange is a ridiculously good pairing. Add some miso to the mix to bring savour to this sweet combo, along with a scattering of toasted sesame seeds, and you have something very special going on. Don't over season the carrots before you roast them – the miso is very salty and savoury, so wait to taste the dish before you reach for the salt.

Preheat the oven to 200°C (Gas Mark 6).

Peel the carrots and roll-cut them into 4-cm pieces. To do this, cut the carrot at an angle to cut off a chunk at one end. Now roll the carrot to quarter-turn it, then cut at the same angle again to cut a nice, chunky wedge shape. Repeat the roll-and-cut process along the length of the carrot. This technique produces interesting shapes with a generous surface area.

Put the carrot chunks into a roasting tray with the sesame oil and orange juice and toss. Season lightly with salt. Cover the tray tightly with foil and roast for 25 minutes.

Remove the foil and mix in the miso. Return the tray to the oven, uncovered this time, and roast for another 10 minutes, until the carrot is cooked and the liquid has mostly evaporated.

Stir in the sesame seeds and coriander just before serving.

HASSELBACK SPUDS & CHIMICHURRI

SERVES 4

700g small or medium potatoes
1 tablespoon sunflower oil
5 tablespoons olive oil
salt and pepper

For the chimichurri
1 small shallot
1 garlic clove
large bunch of flat-leaf
   or curly parsley
small bunch of coriander
1 teaspoon dried oregano
1 red chilli, deseeded
2 tablespoons red wine vinegar
olive oil
salt and pepper

Hasselback potatoes are a pain in the arse to prep, but the crispy comb-like edges are worth all the effort, especially when served with chimichurri. This herby Argentinian sauce is perfect for folding through veg straight from the roasting tray or barbecue. Whizz it in a food processor or chop very finely. What you lose in speed you make up in texture.

Preheat the oven to 180°C (Gas Mark 4).

Thinly slice each potato without cutting all the way through, so the potato stays intact at the base. You can do this by eye, or lay the handle of a wooden spoon next to the potato to stop the knife cutting down to the board.

Place the potatoes in a roasting tray, sliced sides facing up. Toss in the sunflower oil and 1 tablespoon of the olive oil and season. Roast for 30 minutes. Remove from the oven and use a heatproof pastry brush to baste the potatoes with the hot oil from the tray. Bake for a further 20–30 minutes, until completely tender in the centres.

While the potatoes cook, make the chimichurri sauce. Put the shallot, garlic, herbs, chilli and vinegar into the bowl of a food processor. Whizz together adding a steady stream of the remaining olive oil until you have a thick pesto-like sauce. Season with salt and pepper.

As soon as the potatoes come out of the oven, put them into a bowl with the sauce and toss together. Leave to stand for a few minutes before serving.

PRITCHMMUS HUMMUS

MAKES 300G

100g dried chickpeas
1½ tablespoons tahini
4 roasted garlic cloves
zest and juice of ½ a lemon
smoked paprika (optional)
extra virgin olive oil
salt and pepper

A lovely Middle Eastern treat. This is my go-to dip – every vegan likes hummus, right? I use dried chickpeas as I find they have a much better texture and flavour than canned, but you could easily substitute a 400g can of chickpeas and the result will be perfectly acceptable. Roasting the garlic gives this version a delicious smoky flavour. It's easy to make – put whole, peeled garlic cloves into a little roasting tin and cover them with rapeseed oil. Roast them at 220°C (Gas Mark 7) for 30-40 minutes. Couldn't be easier!

Put the dried chickpeas into a bowl, cover them with water and leave to soak overnight.

Drain the soaked chickpeas, transfer to a pan, cover with twice the amount of water and bring to a boil. Once boiling, lower the heat and simmer, covered, for about an hour. Set aside to cool.

Put the cooled chickpeas into the bowl of a food processor with the tahini, garlic, lemon zest and juice and smoked paprika, if using. Drizzle in about a tablespoon of olive oil and blitz. The mixture can be a bit tricky to blend because it sticks to the sides of the bowl. Using a spatula, keep scraping it from the sides into the middle of the bowl, blitzing and adding extra olive oil until you reach your desired consistency. Season well.

PRITCHAMOLE GUACAMOLE

MAKES 200G

2 avocados
1 tomato
juice of 1 lime
pinch of smoked paprika
pinch of chili flakes
salt and pepper

Guacamole is indispensible. It's great as a dip; it's just the thing to add to any kind of wrap or sandwich; you can load it on crisps, tortilla chips, raw veg; add it to a salad...

Put the avocados, tomato, lime juice, paprika and chilli flakes into a bowl. Grab a potato masher and mash away at the mixture until you have a nice scoopable paste. Season with sea salt and pepper.

Pictured on page 173

 PRITCHALSA SALSA

MAKES 300G

1 red onion, chopped
250g tomatoes, chopped
1 green chilli, finely chopped
1 garlic clove, finely chopped
handful of fresh coriander,
   chopped
juice of 1 lime
glug of extra virgin olive oil
salt and pepper

Tomatoes have a delicate, inviting sweetness. The freshness of coriander and lime here really lifts their flavour, and chilli gives this salsa a nice kick. Chop the tomato and onion into small or large chunks, depending on how you like your salsa.

Put the chopped onion and tomato into a bowl. Add the green chilli, garlic, coriander and lime juice and a good glug of olive oil and mix together. Season to taste. Serve up next to your hummus.

Pictured on page 173

VEGAN MAYO

MAKES 250ML

125ml soya milk
1 teaspoon cider vinegar
1 tablespoon lemon juice
½ teaspoon Dijon mustard
up to 250ml olive oil
Himalayan salt

Who doesn't like mayo? I remember visiting Amsterdam when I was younger and they served their fries with mayo, and I thought WTF?!?! But it was nice! So if you're a mayo-with-your-chips (or veggie sticks) kinda person, well... you're welcome! For a paprika mayo, add a teaspoon of smoked paprika to the basic recipe, and for a garlic mayo, add a little crushed garlic to taste (see page 45). And if you like a touch of sweetness to your mayo, you could mix in a tiny bit of maple syrup.

Put the milk, vinegar, lemon juice and mustard into the bowl of a food processor and season with salt. Whizz it all up and, while the motor is still running, gradually pour in the olive oil in a slow, steady stream, stopping when the mixture is thick, emulsified and resembles mayonnaise. Store in an airtight container in the fridge for up to 3 days.

SWEET STUFF and BELLY MAKERS

I used to have a really sweet tooth but prefer the savoury stuff now. Having said that I love the odd treat. These tend to come out at the weekend when I've got mates round.

HEDGEHOG HOMAGE ICE CREAM

SERVES 4

4 ripe bananas, sliced
2 tablespoons cocoa powder
50g hazelnuts, toasted
   and chopped
1 tablespoon raw cacao nibs
small pinch of sea salt (optional)
4 vegan ice cream cones

There is a beach café at Porthchapel in Cornwall that's famous for serving a post-surf pick-me-up called The Hedgehog. It is ice cream covered in clotted cream and rolled in shards of toasted nuts. This is a dairy-free tribute to that inspired creation. You can add 2 tablespoons of nut butter into the ice cream mix if you like. Or omit the cocoa powder and add a handful of frozen berries instead.

Lay the banana slices on a tray and freeze overnight.

When fully frozen, pop the bananas into a food processor with the cocoa powder and blend together until the mixture is smooth and creamy. This may take a few minutes, depending on the oomph of your food processor. You may need to scrape down the sides of the bowl to push the banana back down towards the blades a few times. Transfer the mixture to a tub, pop on a lid and freeze for at least 30 minutes before serving.

Mix the chopped hazelnuts and cacao nibs in a shallow bowl and add a small pinch of sea salt if you are feeling hip.

Top the cones with generous scoops of ice cream. Press and turn the scoops in the nut mix until completely coated. Eat immediately.

RUM-ROASTED PINEAPPLE WITH COCONUT CREAM

SERVES 4

For the rum-roasted pineapple
120g light brown sugar
150ml water
2 shots of dark rum
½ vanilla pod, split
1 star anise
10 black peppercorns
seeds from 4 cardamom pods
3 slices of fresh ginger
1 large pineapple, skin sliced
off and eyes removed, then
cut into 4 large wedges with
the core removed

For the coconut cream
400ml can coconut milk
2 tablespoons icing sugar

As retro as a glass of Malibu. To be eaten in your board shorts, or with a parrot on your shoulder (obviously).

Put the can of coconut milk in the fridge the night before. While you're there, put a mixing bowl in the freezer.

Preheat the oven to 160°C (Gas Mark 3).

Place the sugar, water, rum and spices in a saucepan. Bring to a simmer and cook gently over low heat until the sugar has dissolved. Remove from the heat and set aside.

Place the pineapple in a roasting tray and spoon over the spiced syrup. Roast for 40 minutes, basting with the spiced syrup every 10 minutes or so, until completely tender.

Meanwhile, prepare the coconut cream. Gently remove the can of coconut milk from the fridge without shaking it and open it carefully. The fat solids should have split away from the liquid and risen to the top. Carefully spoon out the fat (save the liquid to use in smoothies or juices).

Remove the cold bowl from the freezer. Add the coconut fat and whisk with an electric whisk on high speed for 5 minutes until whipped and creamy. Whisk in the sugar. Transfer the bowl to the fridge until ready to serve.

Serve the pineapple warm, with the dark syrup from the roasting tray spooned over and a blob of coconut cream on the side.

MALT LOAF

SERVES 8

sunflower oil, for greasing
220ml black tea
150g malt extract
100g light brown
  muscovado sugar
125g raisins, chopped
50g prunes, chopped
50g dried figs, chopped
2 tablespoons ground chia seeds
250g wholemeal plain flour
½ tablespoon baking powder
small pinch of sea salt

The leading brand of malt loaf is well beloved by long distance cyclists. I needed a vegan substitute that would give me the necessary hit of fuel I need to keep going though the most gruelling stretches. This is what I came up with, and it does the job very well. Chia seeds are a cake-loving vegan's gift from the gods. When you soak them in liquid, they become gelatinous, which makes them an excellent binder in cakes in place of eggs.

Preheat the oven to 180°C (Gas Mark 4). Oil a 20 x 10cm loaf tin and line it with baking paper.

Place the tea, malt extract and sugar in a saucepan. Heat gently until the sugar has dissolved. Set aside.

Add the fruit and chia seeds to the tea and leave to soak for 30 minutes.

Sift the flour and baking powder together into a large bowl. Add the salt. Gently fold in both the fruit mixture and the malt mixture until completely combined.

Transfer the batter to the loaf tin. Smooth and level out the top using the back of a spoon. Bake for 30 minutes, then remove the tin from the oven and cover the top with kitchen foil to prevent burning. Return the tin to the oven and bake for a further 20 minutes or until firm.

Leave to cool in the tin, then turn out the loaf and wrap it in greaseproof paper. The malt loaf is best left to mature for a few days before serving.

VICTORIA ORANGE SPONGE

SERVES 8–10

For the sponge layers
100g apple puree
200ml unsweetened soya milk
80ml rapeseed oil
15ml cider vinegar
20ml orange essence
300g self-raising flour
½ teaspoon baking powder
165g caster sugar
½ teaspoon salt
zest of 1 unwaxed orange,
    to serve

For the marmalade icing
40g vegan margarine
100g icing sugar, sifted,
    plus extra for dusting
1–2 tablespoons marmalade

Introducing the classic Vicky sponge but with a hint of orange. It don't half lift the cake and give it that nice zesty kick – you can smell it from Seville. Put the cake on a cake board for a professional touch, or just use a serving plate if you prefer. If you don't have orange essence, use the grated zest of one large unwaxed orange instead, but make sure it is unwaxed as waxed citrus fruits aren't vegan.

Preheat the oven to 160°C (Gas Mark 3). Cut 2 circles from baking paper to fit into the bases of 2 × 18cm round cake tins and add them to the tins.

Put the apple puree into a bowl or jug and blitz it with a stick blender until smooth. Set aside.

Pour the soya milk into a large jug and add the oil, vinegar and orange essence. Mix well with a whisk and set aside. You want to let the wet ingredients curdle, as this makes for a lighter, airier sponge.

Sift the flour and baking powder into a mixing bowl. Add the sugar and salt. Mix the dry ingredients together well with a spoon, ensuring there are no lumps.

Add the apple sauce to the wet ingredients and stir. Now add the wet mixture to the dry ingredients and gently mix using a figure of 8 movement. Ensure they are combined, but don't overmix. Scrape down the sides of the bowl with a spatula.

Recipe continued overleaf

Recipe continued

Split the batter equally between the prepared tins – weigh them to make sure they are equal, and adjust as necessary. Then tap each tin gently on your work surface to release any air bubbles. Smooth out the surfaces with a palette knife to ensure they are flat.

Bake in the centre of the oven for about 30 minutes, until golden. To check the cakes are done, very gently prod them – they should be firm and spring back to shape. Leave to cool in the tins for no more than 5 minutes, then insert a palette knife between tin and cake and carefully manoeuvre it around edge of cake to make ensure it is free. Turn out the cake layers onto separate wire racks. Double flip the cakes to keep them upright so they don't crack. Leave to cool.

To make the icing, whisk the margarine and icing sugar until light. Then add the marmalade and whisk briefly.

Pick up a cooling rack with a cake layer sitting on it in one hand, place your other palm gently on top of the cake, then turn over the wire rack with a confident, swift motion to transfer the cake layer onto your palm. Align a cake board to the exposed base of the cake, then turn the cake layer over again so that it is sitting upright on the cake board.

Spread the filling on top of the bottom layer of the cake and carefully place the remaining sponge layer on top. When ready to show, generously dust the top with icing sugar using a clean sieve and sprinkle with orange zest.

WARM WELSH CAKES WITH BAKED PLUMS

SERVES 2

For the plums
½ vanilla pod or 1 teaspoon
    vanilla extract
600g plums, halved
1 cinnamon stick
a grating of nutmeg
3 tablespoons maple syrup
zest and juice of ½ orange

For the Welsh cakes
150g self-raising flour, sifted,
    plus extra for dusting
pinch of salt
pinch of mixed spice
50g caster sugar
70g vegan butter or margarine
70g currants
3 tablespoons almond milk
sunflower or vegetable oil,
    for frying

I had to get this nod to my home country in! Welsh cakes are griddled on the hob rather than baked in the oven – give them a go. Adding the plums just makes this pud properly homegrown.

Preheat the oven to 200°C (Gas Mark 6). Scrape out the seeds from the vanilla pod, if using, with the back of a knife.

Place the plums in a snug-fitting roasting tin. Throw in the cinnamon stick, a cautious grating of nutmeg and the vanilla extract or seeds and pod. Tip in the maple syrup, orange zest and juice. Mix. Bake for 20 minutes, or until the plums are soft and beginning to collapse.

Meanwhile, make the Welsh cakes. Add the flour, salt, mixed spice and sugar to a mixing bowl and rub in the butter with your fingertips until the mixture resembles fine breadcrumbs. Stir in the currants and add the milk. Gently bring together into a dough, but don't knead or overwork it.

Transfer to a floured surface and roll out to 5mm thick. Using a 6-cm round fluted pastry cutter, stamp out as many circles as you can, re-rolling the waste dough until you can't make anymore. You should get at least 8 dough circles.

Heat a heavy-based frying pan with a tablespoon of oil. Fry the cakes over medium heat for 3–4 minutes on each side, until golden and slightly risen. Serve warm with the warm baked plums.
Pictured overleaf

SUMMER PUDDING
SERVES 6

sunflower oil, for greasing
8 slices of good-quality white
   bread, crusts removed
250g strawberries, sliced,
   plus extra to serve
100g blackcurrants or
   redcurrants, plus extra
   to serve
100g cherries, pitted
150g raspberries,
   plus extra to serve
2 tablespoons water
3 tablespoons caster sugar
2 tablespoons elderflower
   cordial
coconut cream or Hedgehog
   Homage Ice Cream (see page
   178) to serve (optional)

To some this classic pud is nothing more than a glorified fruit sandwich, but I personally think it's so much more than the sum of its parts. There's no reason why you can't make it with autumn fruits – try using blackberries, damsons, grated apple and pear instead.

Lightly oil a 1-litre pudding basin and line it with clingfilm. Leave some clingfilm overhanging the sides to cover the top of the bowl later.

Cut 1 slice of bread into a rough circle and place it into the bottom of the pudding bowl. Use 5 slices to line the inside of the bowl, ensuring they overlap so there are no gaps.

Place the fruit in a saucepan with the measured water and sugar. Cook over low heat for 3–4 minutes without stirring. You want the fruit to start releasing its juices but not soften too much. Remove from the heat and gently stir in the elderflower cordial. Leave to stand for 5 minutes.

Tip the warm fruit and all the liquid from the saucepan into the bread-lined pudding basin. Use the final slices of bread to form a top. Lift the overhanging clingfilm up and over the bowl to cover.

Sit the pudding bowl in a shallow tray (to catch any juices). Place a saucer on top of the pudding, then sit a heavy weight (something more substantial than a can of beans) on top of that, to weigh down and press the pudding. Transfer to the fridge to chill overnight.

Turn out onto a platter in one impressive piece and serve topped with extra fruit and coconut or ice cream, if liked.

MAPLE, ORANGE and CHOCOLATE BAKLAVA

SERVES 6-8

150g dates, chopped
100g almonds
100g walnuts
100g pistachio nuts
zest of 1 orange
2 tablespoon cacao powder
½ teaspoon ground cinnamon
small pinch of salt
12 sheets of filo pasty
light olive oil

For the syrup
75ml fresh orange juice
75ml water
100ml maple syrup
100g caster sugar
seeds from 6 cardamom pods

Yes, this one is full of pricey ingredients, but just one small piece is so sweet and rich that a little goes a long way. It was a good day when I realized you can use olive oil instead of butter for brushing filo pastry sheets to make vegan baklava. Don't use too much, though, to avoid the final dish feeling greasy. If you like, use melted vegan butter instead.

Preheat the oven to 180°C (Gas Mark 4). Cover the dates in a bowl with boiling water and soak for 10 minutes.

Meanwhile, put the nuts into the bowl of a food processer and pulse until coarsely chopped. Transfer to a bowl.

Drain the dates and add to the nuts with the orange zest, cacao, cinnamon and a small pinch of salt. Mix well.

Lay a sheet of pastry in a small baking tray. Brush lightly with olive oil. Lay over 3 more sheets, oiling between each. Spread over half the nut mixture and top with 4 more sheets of oiled pastry. Spread the remaining nut mixture on top and finish with 4 sheets of oil-brushed pastry.

Cut into diamond shapes and bake for 30-40 minutes or until the pastry is cooked and flaky.

While the baklava cooks, make the syrup. Place the orange juice, water, maple syrup and sugar in a saucepan with the cardamom seeds. Simmer gently for 10 minutes.

When the baklava is ready, tip the sweet syrup evenly over the top. Leave to soak for a few hours before serving.

CHOCOLATE CUPCAKES

MAKES 20

For the cupcakes
350ml unsweetened soya milk
15ml apple cider vinegar
330g white sugar
100g vegan baking margarine
300g plain flour
1 teaspoon bicarbonate of soda
80g cocoa powder
½ teaspoon salt
½ teaspoon instant coffee
  granules

For the icing
75g cocoa powder
500g icing sugar
100g vegetable shortening
125ml unsweetened soya milk

I managed to fool the WI with these bad boys. If I can convince the queens of baking that these vegan cupcakes are 'the real thing', then they clearly must be delicious!

Preheat the oven to 180°C (Gas Mark 4). Line cupcake tins with 20 paper cupcake cases.

Put the soya milk and vinegar into a jug and give the mixture a good whisk to combine.

Put the sugar and margarine into a bowl and cream together with a hand blender until the mixture is soft and smooth. Set aside.

Sift the flour, bicarbonate of soda and cocoa powder into a bowl. Add the salt and coffee granules. Mix well with a whisk, ensuring there are no lumps.

Tip the dry mixture into the creamed mixture. Pour in the soya milk mixture. Fold the dry ingredients into the wet using a figure of 8 motion. The mixture will seem dry but will loosen quickly – try not to over-mix it. Scrape down the sides of the bowl with a spatula.

Using a small metal spoon (like a soup spoon), put a rounded spoonful of batter into each case – too much will cause the cake to rise over the top and spill out of the cases. If you want to be a perfectionist you could weigh each filled case to ensure uniform cupcakes! Bake in the centre of the

Recipe continued overleaf

Recipe continued

oven for about 25 minutes or until the cakes spring back when gently poked. Leave to cool completely in the tins before decorating.

To make the icing, sift the cocoa and sugar into a mixing bowl. Transfer to a food processor and add the shortening. Combine the mixture, gradually incorporating the soya milk until your icing has the desired consistency – pliable, but not sloppy.

You can decorate your cupcakes with icing in any way you like – just let your artistic side guide you. If you're convinced you don't have one, follow the guidelines below to get you going.

Transfer the icing to a piping bag. For the whippy look, use a wide open plain round nozzle. Make a blob of icing in the middle of 1 cupcake. Then, starting at the outside edge of the cake and working towards the centre, pipe a series of overlapping concentric circles. When you reach the centre, finish with a tiny push down, then lift up the nozzle.

Alternatively, for a rose icing finish, use a 2D nozzle. Create a small blob in the middle of a cupcake, then, working towards the edge of the cake, pipe a series of overlapping concentric circles and finish with a little flick.

VEGAN CHEESECAKE

SERVES 10

For the base
300g oat biscuits
(I use Hobnobs)
1 tablespoon coconut oil

For the filling
600g vegan cream cheese
160g coconut cream
few drops of vanilla extract
50g caster sugar
1 × 6.5g sachet vegan gelatine

For the topping
6 black-coloured biscuits
(I use Oreos)

This really is naughty, but oh-so nice! If you're worrying about your love handles, I suggest you steer well clear, but once in a blue moon, why not? Every time I've made this cake it hasn't even lasted a few minutes. Every piece was munched, with happy faces all round. It's not difficult to make, and the ingredients are easy to find. Most people who become vegan very quickly discover the brands of biscuit that are vegan-friendly (funny, that), and vegan cream cheese is available in most supermarkets now.

First make the base. Empty the oat biscuits into a bowl and crush them with the end of a rolling pin until the contents of the bowl resembles a crumble topping.

Mix in the coconut oil (melt it first if it has set) to make the biscuit base a little damp. Pack the mixture into a 21-cm springform cake tin or loose-bottomed cake tin, so when the cake is ready you can lift it out easily without making a mess and ruining your work of art. Grab a spoon and compress the mixture so you have a flat base, then put the tin into the fridge and leave to set. An hour should be enough.

To make the filling, put the vegan cream cheese into a mixing bowl. Add the coconut cream, vanilla extract and caster sugar. Mix well.

Recipe continued overleaf

Recipe continued

Dissolve the vegan gelatine in very little hot water (just a few millilitres) and add a little of this solution to the mixing bowl – avoid adding too much or the filling will become watery. Now use a whisk to fluff up the ingredients into a nice paste with a spreadable consistency.

Spread the filling mixture evenly across the biscuit base. Transfer to the fridge and leave to set. This could take 3 hours.

Before you remove the cheesecake from the fridge, grab your black-coloured biscuits or Oreos and remove the cream with a knife (if necessary) and discard it. Put the black biscuits into the bowl of a blender and whizz to a fine dust.

Sprinkle the black dust over your cheesecake, then carefully remove it from the tin and shove it down yer gob.

GUEST CHEF: SARA WILLIAMS, AQUAFABA PAVLOVAS

SERVES 6

fruit topping of your choice
(optional, we used 1 mango,
roughly chopped, 1 papaya,
roughly chopped, the seeds
from 2 passionfruit, and the
zest of 1 unwaxed lime)

For the coconut cream
chilled coconut cream (chill a
400ml can of full-fat coconut
milk overnight, then carefully
scoop out the thick, white
cream from the top, reserving
the coconut water beneath
to use in a smoothie if liked)
4 tablespoons icing sugar
½ teaspoon vanilla bean paste

For the meringues
100ml liquid from canned
chickpeas (aquafaba)
dash of food colouring
paste (optional)
1 tablespoon lemon juice
1 teaspoon vanilla bean paste
100g granulated sugar

Isn't it amazing that you can make a crisp, light pavlova using chickpea water? Yep, believe it or not, this is possible. Share this pudding with non-vegan friends and blow their minds!

Preheat the oven to 100°C (Gas Mark ¼). Line a large baking sheet with baking paper. Put a bowl into the freezer to chill.

To make the meringues, use a food processor with a balloon whisk (ensure the bowl is scrupulously clean and dry) to whisk the aquafaba and food colouring, if using, for 2 minutes. Add the lemon juice and vanilla bean paste and whisk on full speed for 5–20 minutes, until more than doubled in volume.

Now incorporate the sugar, 1 teaspoon at a time, with the whisk still moving. You should have a beautiful fluffy mixture and it should stay in the bowl when you turn it upside down.

Pack the mixture into a piping bag and pipe 12-cm swirls onto the baking sheet. Bake for 2–3 hours – a longer bake results in a crispier meringue – then leave to cool on the baking sheet. Put the food processor whisk in the freezer to chill for the coconut cream.

Meanwhile, add the coconut cream into the chilled bowl and whisk until fluffy. Add the icing sugar and vanilla bean paste and whisk again for 1–2 minutes to incorporate. Use immediately or store in the fridge in an airtight container.

When ready to serve, spoon the coconut cream over each meringue, then top with fresh fruit, if using.

RICE PUDDING WITH BLUEBERRY COMPOTE

SERVES 4

For the rice pudding
400ml can coconut milk
400ml water
125g risotto rice
1 teaspoon vanilla extract
50g caster sugar (or 75g if you
    have a sweet tooth like me)

For the compote
5 tablespoons water
50g caster sugar
125g blueberries

The king of puddings! This one brings back many childhood memories, especially of school. A dollop of strawberry jam in the middle or some vegan chocolate buttons will bring out the kid in you.

Empty the coconut milk into a saucepan, then add the water (as you need equal amounts of water and coconut milk, use the empty can to measure the water and swill out all residue of coconut milk from the can when you tip the water into the pan). Stir in the rice and vanilla essence. Set the pan over medium-low heat and mix in the caster sugar. Bring the mixture to a simmer and let simmer for approximately 10–15 minutes, until the rice is cooked.

To make the compote, put the water into a saucepan with the caster sugar. Set the pan over medium-low heat and add the berries. Simmer for 5–10 minutes, until you have a gooey compote.

INDEX

ACKNOWLEDGEMENTS

There is no 'I' in the word team. And never is that expression truer in relation to the creation of a cookery book or indeed the TV series it accompanies. *Dirty Vegan* the TV series has been made by One Tribe TV, run by Dale Templar and Owen Gay, who have supported and guided me throughout, together with their talented, hardworking and dedicated production team. Special thanks go to:
Luke Lovell
Matt Waddleton
Chloe Lewis
Cameron Howells
Alex Rowe
Jonathon Aiken
Sonny Mackay
Isa Campbell
Sam Webb
Francesca Barbieri
Val Rogers
David Stevens
Jonny Doggett
Jessie Anderson
Olivia Vanpuyenbroek
...and the final post team at The Dog House.

The series was commissioned thanks to the absolute faith of Julian Carey, together with the BBC Wales in-house TV commissioning and online teams.

Likewise thanks to all the contributors and off screen helpers who supported the production and inspired me to create so many exciting recipes particularly everyone at the Scarlets Ladies Rugby Team, South and Mid Wales Cave Rescue Team, Meas Y Gwendreath School, Glamorgan Federation of the Women's Institute, Cae Tan Organic Farm, The Tidy Kitchen, Naturally Kind Food, Cardiff Met University Department of Food Science and Technology, Naturally Kind Food, Murton Hall – Swansea and Gower Methodist Circuit, The Brecon Beacons National Park Authority, and National Diving and Activity Centre.

Finally, thanks to Daffodil PR for helping to promote the series and the book and One Tribe Talent Ltd for management support.

Dirty Vegan the book has been a labour of vegan love. Special thanks must go to Rachel Lovell who has steered this project and brought me together with the remarkable team at Octopus Books including Eleanor Maxfield and Pauline Bache, designers Emma and Alex Smith and the amazing photography teams of Chris Terry and Jamie Orlando Smith, as well as food stylist Phil Mundy and props stylist Olivia Wardle. And last but not least, a special shout out to chef Rob Andrew who helped me pull together all these fantastic recipes in an incredibly short space of time.

Thanks also to Adrian Rooke and our staff at SWYD for keeping the businesses rocking while I've been away. My mother and father for always being supportive and forever entertaining me with their comic genius. My brothers Trigg and Duchess, sister-in-law Annie-mall and my niece Mia Seren.

Thank you to Scott Carey for online content, filming and for calling that meeting; to James Threlfall and Pete Pickford for my YouTube show; and to Mark Whittle and Simon Webb for all things triathlon and fitness.

A special thanks to my fiancée Ciara Dunne who was by my side in my darker days, continued to support me and convince me not to give up and persuaded me to get help. I am now in a very good place, thank you and I love you.

Thank you everybody. If there's anyone I've missed out, I apologise but you all know what my brain's like!